Bold Women
in
Indiana History

LOUISE
HILLERY

2016
Mountain Press Publishing Company
Missoula, Montana

Library of Congress Cataloging-in-Publication Data

Names: Hillery, Louise, 1946- author.
Title: Bold women in Indiana history / Louise Hillery.
Description: Missoula, Montana : Mountain Press Publishing Company, 2016. |
  Series: Bold women series | Includes bibliographical references and index.
Identifiers: LCCN 2015042570 | ISBN 9780878426553 (pbk. : alk. paper)
Subjects: LCSH: Women–Indiana–Biography–Juvenile literature. | Women
  heroes–Indiana–Biography–Juvenile literature. |
  Women–Indiana–History–Juvenile literature. |
  Indiana–Biography–Juvenile literature. | Indiana–History–Juvenile
  literature.
Classification: LCC CT3262.I5 H55 2016 | DDC 920.7209772–dc23
LC record available at http://lccn.loc.gov/2015042570

PRINTED IN THE UNITED STATES

MP Mountain Press
PUBLISHING COMPANY
P.O. Box 2399 • Missoula, MT 59806 • 406-728-1900
800-234-5308 • info@mtnpress.com
www.mountain-press.com

This book is dedicated to the bold girls of Indiana, both young and old. Don't let anyone tell you what a girl can't do.

ACKNOWLEDGMENTS

My personal thanks to the staff and volunteers of the Indiana Historical Society, the West Chester Historical Society, Madison Jefferson County Public Library, Indiana State Library, Lew Wallace Study and Museum, Cambridge City Public Library and Overbeck Museum, Madam Walker Theater, Limberlost State Historic Site, Gene Stratton-Porter State Historic Site, and Calumet Regional Archives. Much appreciation also to A'Lelia Bundles for sharing her knowledge and materials from the Walker Family Archives. I am especially grateful to Phyllis Mattheis and Marsha Ringenberg Wright, who shared their personal memories and family artifacts. I also want to thank the members of the Scribblers writing group for their encouragement and suggestions. And special thanks to editor Gwen McKenna, who knew when to be a visionary and when to be a nitpicker.

CONTENTS

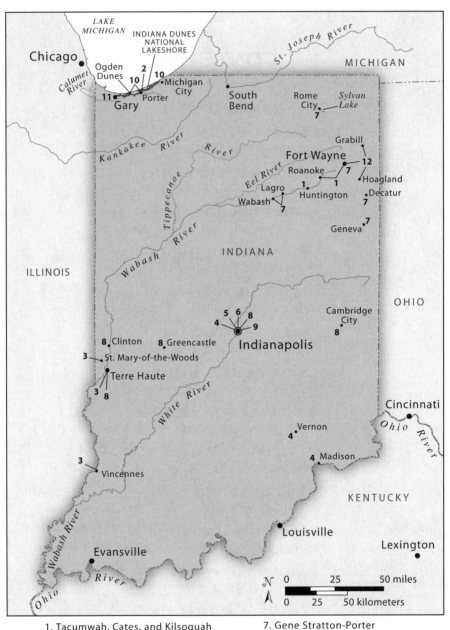

1. Tacumwah, Cates, and Kilsoquah
2. Marie Bailly
3. Mother Théodore Guérin
4. Sarah Bolton
5. Zerelda Wallace
6. Lillian Thomas Fox
7. Gene Stratton-Porter
8. The Overbeck sisters
9. Madam C. J. Walker
10. Dorothy Buell
11. Vivian Carter
12. Margaret Ray Ringenberg

INTRODUCTION

When I was a teacher, students would sometimes ask me why there were so few women in their history books. Looking into this question on a local level, I discovered numerous interesting, original, and bold Hoosier women who helped make Indiana what it is today. Of these, I chose twelve of the most representative and most compelling life stories.

First you will meet several prominent women of the Miami tribe, one of the original peoples of Indiana. Tacumwah was an influential leader and a very successful trader who became the wealthiest Miami woman of her day. Cates, Tacumwah's granddaughter, was the wife of one tribal chief and the mother of another. And Kilsoquah became famous as the last full-blooded Miami Indian to live in Indiana. Surviving to age 105, she shared stories of her Indian ancestors and her memories of Indiana from pre-statehood warfare to the modern age.

Marie Bailly, part Ottawa Indian and part French, and her husband Joseph were the first settlers in northwest Indiana. With her fur-trader husband, she endured many hardships and raised cultured and educated children under frontier conditions. As a mixed-race person in a time of strict racial divisions, her struggles still resonate today.

Mother Théodore Guérin, now known as Saint Theodora, crossed the raging Atlantic Ocean in poor health to lead the Sisters of Providence to Indiana. Triumphing over misfortunes, poverty, local distrust, and opposition from leaders in their own church, these brave nuns established schools, orphanages, and medical clinics, as well as St. Mary-of-the-Woods College.

1

Sarah Bolton, known as Indiana's pioneer poet, published her first poem at age fourteen and continued to write well-loved verses throughout her life.

When the state legislature snubbed Zerelda Wallace's petition for controls on liquor sales because the women who signed it were not voters, Zerelda became a suffragist, determined to win the right to vote for women. Her peacemaking ways brought together warring factions in the suffrage movement.

Born a free black woman before the Civil War, Lillian Thomas Fox was the first female African American journalist in Indiana and the first black writer employed by a white daily newspaper in the state. With Dr. Beulah Porter, she formed the Colored Women's Improvement Club. When tuberculosis was killing black citizens and the public hospitals would not treat them, the club ran tuberculosis clinics and sponsored medical training for black nurses.

Many people recognize the name of Gene Stratton-Porter, author of romance novels in the "Golden Age of Indiana Literature." Less well known are her serious nature studies, her developments in the field of nature photography, her advocacy for environmental protection, and her later career as a Hollywood film producer.

The six daughters of the Overbeck family were raised to believe they were special, and they were encouraged to use their artistic talents for useful purposes. Four of the sisters created an art pottery business that made them famous, and their pots, vases, and figurines are still highly valued.

Sarah Breedlove, later known as Madam C. J. Walker, was born in Louisiana to two former slaves. Orphaned by age eight, married at fourteen, a mother at seventeen, and a widow at twenty, she started a business when she could barely read and write. To secure a better future for her daughter, she started her own line of hair-care products, educated herself, and became the foremost black businesswoman in the United States.

Dorothy Buell and her husband were ready to relax into their golden years when they stopped in at a meeting about preserving the Indiana sand dunes. She joined and eventually took over a campaign to save the state's unique lakeshore from industrialization. Fighting powerful forces, this proper little lady assembled a coalition that still serves as a model for environmental activism.

Vivian Carter was running a record shop and hosting a radio program when she started a recording company that paved the way for black musicians to be heard by white audiences. Although her poor choices of business partners brought her company down as fast as it had risen to the top, she left a permanent mark on the history of rock music.

Margaret Ray Ringenberg was fascinated by airplanes from the age of seven. After high school, she was studying for her pilot's license when World War II broke out. Answering her country's call, she served in the newly formed Women's Airforce Service Pilots program. After the war, this spunky lady continued to fly, working as a flight instructor and a competitive racer.

Each of these women had her own talents and her own ideas about how to make the world a better place. What they had in common were courage and determination, enough to bring their ideas to life. These are some of the many bold women who helped make the Hoosier state what it is today.

Kilsoquah (1810–1915) and her son, Anthony Revarre, better known as Tony Loon. Photo taken 1910. —Courtesy Miami County Historical Society

TACUMWAH, CATES, AND KILSOQUAH

Daughters of the Miami Tribe

Before Europeans came to Indiana, it was home to the Miami, Potawatomi, Wea, Delaware, Kickapoo, and Shawnee peoples. French fur traders came before 1700, then British soldiers, and finally American settlers. After Indiana became a state in 1816, Americans wanted to buy up Indian land, so the government forced the Native Americans to relocate to reservations west of the Mississippi River. But the Miami resisted, and several bold Miami women played a big part in securing a permanent place in Indiana for many Miami families. Among these women were Tacumwah, Cates, and Kilsoquah, all of whom were members of a prominent Miami clan that included many chiefs and other leaders.

Until most of the tribe was removed from the state in the 1840s, the Miami made up the majority of the Native American population in Indiana. The Miami, an agricultural people, generally set up their villages near a water source. They grew mostly corn but also squashes, beans, and melons. The Miami were also ardent traders, exchanging goods with other tribes and, later, with Europeans. With the Europeans they traded animal skins and food for guns, tools, liquor, and other manufactured items.

In the early days, the Miami lived in rounded lodges made of bent wooden poles covered with bark or woven mats, but by the late 1700s most Miami families resided in wooden cabins. A Miami village would also include one or more larger, more permanent log structures known as longhouses. These buildings were used for council meetings, seasonal ceremonies, and other gatherings. The Miami spent little time indoors, however, even in the winter.

As in most tribes, village responsibilities were divided between the sexes. The women did most of the farming while the men mostly hunted and acted as protectors. The women also took care of the food preparation—shelling, chopping, butchering, cooking, and sun drying. Making things like clothing, pottery, and woven mats was part of the feminine domain as well, as was child care. In addition, women as well as children gathered wild fruits, nuts, and medicinal plants. In the winter, the men hunted bison and other large game for meat to supplement the stored food that the women had prepared.

Unlike some tribes, however, the Miami had both male and female chiefs, or leaders, although their duties were different. A male war chief supervised conflicts and battles between the Miami and other tribes, while the female war chief, or chieftess, made sure the warriors had the supplies they needed; she also led the women's war songs and dances, performed in support of the fighters. There were also civil chiefs in each village—the male civil chief watched over the village and mediated any problems within the community, while the civil chieftess was in charge of preparations for feasts and festivals.

Although the Miami did not have royalty in the European sense, leadership roles were to some extent inherited, so the daughters of a high-ranking chief were sometimes referred to as princesses by the Europeans. Coming from a respected family, these girls were held in high esteem within their tribe. One of them might grow up to be a chieftess in the village, but only if she showed leadership ability.

Here you will learn the stories of several important Miami women, all related to the famous war chief Me-she-kin-o-quah, or Little Turtle. First you will meet Ta-cum-wah (c. 1740–98), whose name in Miami means Parakeet. She was the older half-sister of Chief Little Turtle. Next comes Po-con-go-quah (c. 1810–49), or Catherine Richardville, also known as Cates, who was Tacumwah's granddaughter and

6

Little Turtle's great-niece. Finally, you will read about Kil-so-quah (1810–1915), translated as Setting Sun, granddaughter of Chief Little Turtle; when she died at age 105, she was believed to have been the last full-blooded Miami Indian in Indiana.

Growing up as Miami girls, all of these women would have had similar experiences. Village life involved much work, especially in the warmer months. Children were taught at a young age that everyone in the clan was expected to help out. The younger children began by helping their mothers with simple tasks as soon as they were able. Older children had their own jobs, usually things like hauling water, helping with the planting and harvesting of crops, and gathering wild foods. Girls, of course, also learned domestic skills such as cooking and weaving, while boys were taught to hunt and to fight. In their early teens, both boys and girls participated in fasting rituals and vision quests, though not together.

When a girl reached maturity in her late teens, she was available for marriage. For the Miami, courtship and marriage amounted to an elaborate exchange of gifts between the families of the bride and groom. Some men had more than one wife at a time. The Miami had a taboo against marrying someone from one's own village, so would-be suitors had to seek partners from another clan or from a different tribe; marriages between Miami women and European men were very common. Divorce was a simple matter of one spouse leaving the other. After a divorce, the children generally stayed with the mother, though the father often remained involved in their upbringing.

When not busy with work, the Miami, children and adults alike, loved to play games. In some games men and women or boys and girls played together while others were played by one or the other sex. Adults, both men and women, particularly enjoyed gambling games. Men and boys often played competitive games that tested their skills.

In the evenings, all the children of the village would sit around the fire listening to the elders tell stories of the past. This was how Miami children learned the history of their people, without books.

Little Turtle, or Meshekinoquah, was born about 1752, before the American Revolution. He was one of the sons of the Miami leader Ac-que-nac-que, or Turtle. His mother may have been a Mohican. Her name is unknown, but she was Turtle's second wife. His first wife, whose name is also unknown, was probably also a Mohican and may have been his second wife's sister. Turtle had had children with her as well, including Pa-can-ne and Tacumwah, both of whom would become tribal leaders.

Although he was the son of a chief, Little Turtle was not automatically a chief himself. For this honor he had to show his courage and leadership. He first showed these qualities in 1780, when a group of French soldiers attacked the main Miami village of Kekionga. Little Turtle gathered up a band of warriors and attacked the French camp at night, killing all but one soldier. Afterward, due to his bravery, Little Turtle was made a war chief of the Miami.

Ten years later, the American army came to northern Indiana to chase the Indians out. Little Turtle's warriors defeated the Americans twice. In 1794 the Miami made peace with the Americans, and Little Turtle helped his people live harmoniously with the white settlers. Over the years he met many important white people, including presidents George Washington, John Adams, and Thomas Jefferson. In 1807 Little Turtle visited the new capital of Washington, D.C., where he saw many things that impressed him, and he concluded that America was a great nation.

In 1812 the Americans were preparing for war with the British. Many Indian leaders, including Shawnee chiefs Te-cum-seh and Ten-skwa-ta-wa ("the Prophet"), were organizing warriors to fight on the British side, but Little Turtle sent a letter to Indiana territorial governor (and future U.S. president) William Henry Harrison, telling him the Miami people would not fight against the United States. Although Little Turtle died in 1812, just as the war began, the United States remembered his loyalty and that of the Miami people. Years later, when the other tribes were removed from Indiana, some Miami families were allowed to stay, including many of Little Turtle's children and grandchildren.

Little Turtle's half-sister, Tacumwah, was a leader in her own right as well as a businesswoman. Her brother Pacanne was chief of Kekionga (which later evolved into the city of Fort Wayne), the largest Miami village. Kekionga and the surrounding area, which Pacanne and his clan owned, was very valuable land, located between rivers that flow north to the Great Lakes and Atlantic Ocean on one side, and rivers that flow south to the Gulf of Mexico on the other side. This eight-mile strip of land was a portage, a place where people transported their belongings and their trade goods. It was here that the family built their trading post.

When Pacanne was away, which he often was, Tacumwah was left in charge of Kekionga. She also ran the trading post, selling goods such as food, furs, and livestock to European traders and her fellow Indians as they passed through. Due to her bloodline and her power, Tacumwah was often referred to as a chieftess, and sometimes even as a "queen," though among the Miami she was simply called a leader. Through the years, she earned enough money and property to become known as the weathiest woman in the tribe.

Around 1757, when she was seventeen, Tacumwah married a French fur trader named Antoine Joseph Drouet de la Richardville (he went by his middle name, Joseph). In those days, French traders were among the first white men in the region that would later become Indiana, and they often married Indian women. Tacumwah and Joseph had four children, including son Jean Baptiste de Richardville, or Pe-she-wa (Wildcat), born in 1761, who became a very important man among the Miami. According to Miami tradition, as the son of the village chief's sister, Peshewa was in line to become the next village chief if he proved himself worthy.

Unfortunately, Joseph was abusive to Tacumwah, and after he took sides against her brother Pacanne, Tacumwah divorced him in 1774. Joseph tried to claim Tacumwah's property in the divorce, but she and Pacanne took him to court and won. Afterward Tacumwah married Joseph's rival, trader Charles Beaubien, and they had a daughter.

When Tacumwah's son Peshewa, or Jean Baptiste, was twelve years old, his father took him to Canada to attend school, where he learned English and French as well as academic subjects. The experience also taught him how to get along in white society. But the boy was bashful, and it was his mother, Tacumwah, who taught him to assert himself. She wanted him to become chief after Pacanne, so she devoted herself to encouraging him to develop his strengths. One day, when Peshewa was a young man of perhaps twenty, he got a chance to demonstrate his worthiness as a chief, and Tacumwah made sure he seized it.

Miami warriors had captured a British man and tied him to a stake in the middle of camp. The elders had decided he should be burned. Tacumwah objected, saying the prisoner was unarmed and had meant no harm, but the elders overruled her. As the warriors prepared to perform the dance of death, Tacumwah retreated to a nearby wooded area with Peshewa. Unseen in the dark, mother and son watched as the dance began. Quietly placing a knife handle in her son's hand, Tacumwah whispered, "When the time is right, jump into the circle and cut his ties." Just as the warriors were lighting the fire, Peshewa rushed in, cut the captive free, pulled him out of the circle, and steered him back to the hiding place. Tacumwah guided the rescued white man into a canoe, hid him under a pile of pelts, and sent him down the Maumee River to safety.

Although the warriors were disappointed, they respected Peshewa's and Tacumwah's courage, and the story was repeated often through the years. Upon the death of his uncle Pacanne in 1815, Peshewa did indeed become civil chief of the Miami. He was known as Chief Richardville. After her son became chief, Tacumwah continued to give him guidance, advising him and participating in council meetings.

Tacumwah also taught her son the trading business, and he was as successful at this occupation as his mother was. When Tacumwah died in the late 1700s, Chief Richardville inherited her wealth, adding to his already considerable prestige and influence. As chief, he knew how to negotiate treaties that protected the interests of the Miami people. The Miami owned some of the best land in the state, which the U.S. government wanted to take over and sell to white settlers. Before the relocation began, however, Chief Richardville and his clan proved that they owned the land and therefore could not be removed. Although he could not save all of his people forever, the chief was able, through various treaty provisions, to secure a private reserve of land for his clan along the St. Mary River.

Chief Jean Baptiste de Richardville died in 1841, at age eighty. Decades later, his grand house on the St. Mary River, the oldest Indian structure in the Midwest, was made into a museum. In 2012 the 1827 home, near today's Huntington, was named a National Historic Landmark.

Chief Richardville's children—Tacumwah's grandchildren—were born into wealth and prestige. Before he became chief, Peshewa had married an Indian woman, probably a Miami, around 1790. Her name was Na-to-ma-quah, and the couple had at least four children. Their youngest daughter was Pe-con-go-quah, or Catherine, called Cates, born in Kekionga about 1810. Cates and her siblings were all educated in Catholic boarding schools in Fort Wayne.

In 1828, Cates married Francis LaFontaine, or To-pe-ah. Like Cates's father, Topeah was half French and half Miami. The couple had seven children. Upon Chief Richardville's death in 1841, Topeah succeeded his father-in-law as chief of the Miami. Cates had inherited her father's luxurious home, and the family moved in. Cates educated her children as she herself had been educated, in Catholic boarding schools.

Thanks to her father's negotiations, when the Miami relocation began in 1846, Cates and her family were among the few Miami who were allowed to stay in Indiana. But while Cates stayed in Huntington with her children, her husband, Chief Topeah, accompanied the evicted groups of his people to the reservation in what is now Kansas. As chief, he wanted to see to it that they arrived safely. He never made it back. On his way home in 1847, Topeah died, though the cause of his death is unknown. The following year, Cates married a wealthy businessman named Francis Laselle, but only three months later, she died. Some of Cates's descendants still live in Indiana.

On the other side of this family tree were the direct descendants of Tacumwah's half-brother Chief Little Turtle. Sometime in the early 1800s, Little Turtle's son Wok-shin-gah, or "Crescent Moon," married Nah-wa-kah-mo-kwa, "Snow Woman," daughter of She-mock-en-ish, or Soldier, an important village chief. The couple lived in a small wood cabin by the forks of the Wabash River, near what is now Huntington. In 1810, in the warm and sunny month of the sandhill cranes (May), a baby girl was born to them. As the granddaughter of two chiefs, the child would be held in high esteem within the tribe. As far as is known, she had no brothers or sisters.

When the baby was ten days old, her parents took her to an elder woman of the village to learn what her name would be, as was the custom. The wisewoman told Crescent Moon and Snow Woman that she had dreamt of beautiful colors in the evening sky. Therefore, she said, the girl's name would be Kil-so-quah, which means "Setting Sun."

When Kilsoquah was born, Indiana was not yet a state, and there were few settlements and no roads in the area. By the time she died at age 105, Kilsoquah had seen a century's worth of changes, including watching nearly everyone in her tribe moved from their homeland to Indian territory in what became Oklahoma. Because she lived into modern times, Kilsoquah's story can help us understand how things changed for the Miami of Indiana.

Even as an adult, Kilsoquah spoke only Miami, having never learned to speak fluent English, and she held on to many tribal customs. Indian women often concerned themselves with maintaining cultural traditions. One of those traditions was storytelling, and Kilsoquah loved to tell stories of her life and her family.

A favorite tale described the time she killed a deer with a small hatchet. One day, Kilsoquah heard dogs barking and hurried over to see what was going on. Some white hunters' dogs had cornered a deer. Kilsoquah sneaked up and killed the deer. The hunters, she said, came and took the slain animal without giving her any meat.

She still had the hatchet in old age and often showed it to visitors as she told the story. She also remembered a treaty meeting that was held in the nearby town of Wabash in 1820, when she was a young girl. Kilsoquah laughed as she told how the Indians were frightened by the loud music the American soldiers played in their camp at night.

Kilsoquah also liked to talk about her grandfather, Little Turtle, though she was only two years old when he died. She said she recalled climbing on his lap to comb his long hair. Throughout her life, Kilsoquah heard stories of her illustrious grandfather's glorious victories in battle and the good things he did for the Miami people.

Kilsoquah's other grandfather, Soldier, also had a story. In 1795 the Miami and other Indians met with General Anthony Wayne at Greenville, Ohio, to make a peace treaty. Over 1,100 Indians, including Chiefs Soldier and Little Turtle, came to the treaty grounds. To celebrate the signing of the treaty, General Wayne passed out peace medals and gifts, one of which was the general's own handmade flag. General Wayne presented this special flag to Chief Soldier, saying, "Keep this flag in sight and as often as you see it, remember we are friends."

"After the death of my grandfather Shemockenish at Thorntown," Kilsoquah said, "the flag came to me [as] his descendant." She treasured this heirloom and kept it carefully for years.

One day, many years later, Kilsoquah's cousin Susan Dixon, another granddaughter of Soldier, asked to borrow the flag to show someone. Susan's clan believed that certain objects could bring them luck, and, unbeknownst to Kilsoquah, Susan intended to keep the flag for that reason. Later, when Kilsoquah asked her cousin to return the flag, Susan told her it had burned up in a fire. Believing the story, Kilsoquah was heartbroken. She would not discover the truth until she was a very old woman.

In 1826, when Kilsoquah was sixteen years old, she married John Owl, son of Miami chief John Owl, and Kilsoquah moved with John to his village along the Eel River. Only a few months after the wedding, John became ill. Within a year he was dead, and Kilsoquah returned to her father's house by the forks of the Wabash River, where she had grown up.

Not long afterward, the U.S. government gave Kilsoquah's father, Crescent Moon, 640 acres of good farmland in Ohio as thanks for his helping with a treaty deal. But Crescent Moon did not want to move his family away from their tribal homeland, so he traded the Ohio land to a white man for 320 acres of forest near Roanoke, Indiana. In 1830 Crescent Moon cleared some trees on his new property, built a log cabin for his family, and started a farm. Kilsoquah lived in the family cabin for most of the rest of her life.

Beginning in 1830, the federal government began its relocation of Midwestern tribes, and most Natives were forced to leave Indiana and go to reservations in the West. But Kilsoquah's clan was one of those allowed to stay because they did not fight against the United States in the War of 1812. Nevertheless, the settlers who soon streamed in disrupted the Miami's traditional way of life, taking parcels of land here and there throughout northeastern Indiana. When Kilsoquah's family was short on money, Crescent Moon sold pieces of his farm to settlers. Later, Kilsoquah would also sell a few parcels. Over time, the original 320 acres would dwindle to 40 acres.

In 1832 Kilsoquah, age twenty-two, married her second husband, Anthony (or Antoine) Revarre. He was half Miami, half French Canadian. His Indian name was Shaw-pe-nom-quah, meaning "Thunderstorm." When they married, Anthony moved to the Roanoke farm with Kilsoquah and her parents. The Revarres had six children, but only two lived beyond infancy. ThJSJe older was a daughter, Wan-nog-quan-quah, meaning "Cold Mist," born around 1845. Her English name was Mary. Not long after the girl's birth, both of Kilsoquah's parents, Crescent Moon and Snow Woman, died. They were buried on the family farm, with no markers.

In 1849, Kilsoquah was pregnant with her son when her husband, Anthony, died suddenly. The boy was born two months after his father's death. He was named Wa-pe-mung-quah, or "White Loon," though he was called Little White Loon because his uncle was Great

White Loon. His English name was Anthony, like his father, but he went by Tony.

Kilosoquah never married again, raising her two children on her own. She sent Mary and Tony to Roanoke Academy, a private school near their home. They both received a good education there.

Around 1875, Mary, age thirty, moved to the Miami reservation in Oklahoma. She married a a white farmer named Taylor and became a teacher in the Indian schools. She and her husband had no children. After Mary left, Kilsoquah did not hear from her for many years. She went to Oklahoma at least once to search for her daughter but could not find her. Meanwhile, Mary had been sending letters to relatives in Indiana, but somehow the letters never got to Kilsoquah. Receiving no replies, Mary concluded that her mother was dead and stopped writing to her.

Kilsoquah's son, Tony, remained on the farm with his mother. He married a white schoolteacher named Millie Downs, who moved into Kilsoquah and Tony's cabin. Millie and Tony had no children, and she died of tuberculosis in 1902. Tony never remarried; he stayed with his mother and took care of her for the rest of her life. He also served as her interpreter, for he spoke English.

Kilsoquah and Tony lived simply on the farm. Kilsoquah made quilts and crafts such as toy canoes and Indian ornaments, while Tony hunted and fished; he also raised hunting dogs for a while. After the family's original cabin burned down in 1896, they built a frame house. Kilsoquah remained healthy enough to do housework, work in the fields, and chop wood well into her nineties.

In 1902, when Kilsoquah was ninety-two years old, something happened that made news thoughout the country. The historic battle flag given to her grandfather Soldier by General Anthony Wayne in 1795 was discovered. After Susan Dixon died, her daughter, needing money, had sold the flag to a local physician, Dr. Perry G. Moore. When Dr. Moore showed the flag to Kilsoquah, she could hardly believe that the flag had not been burned, that her cousin had lied.

As Kilsoquah gently unfolded the bullet-torn flag, tears welled up in her eyes. "This is the flag," she said as her fingers traced the lines of the stitching on the red, white, and blue stripes. In the corner was the insignia, which read, "A. Wayne, Commander in Chief." She folded the flag tenderly, held it to her face, and kissed it as tears trickled down her cheeks. She said to her interpreter, "Tell the doctor I am glad he has got it, for he will take good care of it." After Dr. Moore's death, his daughter donated the famous flag to the Indiana Historical Bureau, so it now belongs to all Hoosiers.

Shortly after the flag story appeared in the newspapers, the people in the Roanoke area realized that Kilsoquah was the oldest Miami Indian in Indiana, and she soon became a local celebrity. Newspapers wrote articles about her, calling her an "Indian princess," and she was invited to be the guest of honor at the 1902 Old Settlers' Day picnic in Allen County. It was the first of many such appearances. Tony would go with his mother to these events to translate for her.

When Kilsoquah was ninety-five, a historian named Jacob Piatt Dunn paid her a visit. Dunn wanted to learn about Indian history and Indian names for a book he was writing. Thanks to Kilsoquah's help, we know what many Miami names mean and how to say them. Dunn's book, called *True Indian Stories*, was published in 1908.

In 1907, when Kilsoquah was ninety-seven years old, she was informed that the town of Columbia City, Indiana, wanted to find and rebury the remains of Kilsoquah's cousin, Chief Coesse, in that city, which was Coesse's home. He had died while visiting Roanoke, so he was buried there, but the site of his grave was unknown. Kilsoquah was the only living person who knew where it was. Dr. Sylvanus Koontz, Kilsoquah's physician and close friend, offered to look for the grave, which Kilsoquah said was near the burial site of her husband, Anthony. She asked Dr. Koontz to bring back the remains of her husband also, so she could rebury them in Greenwood Cemetery, where she herself planned to be buried; she wanted their graves to be side by side.

Even though she had not visited the graves for thirty-six years, Kilsoquah remembered exactly where they were. She told Dr. Kootz and her son, Tony, "Go to the old walnut tree and take thirty-five paces toward the apple trees." The walnut tree had been cut down long ago, but Dr. Koontz and Tony found the stump and measured from there. They found the graves just as Kilsoquah had described, with the objects she said the bodies were buried with: a silver pipe, a silver ring, a gold ring, some china, a headdress ornament, and some other items. The searchers knew they had identified the right graves. They brought everything back, and Coesse and Anthony were reburied in their respective new graves.

With each passing year, Kilsoquah's fame grew. Some 6,000 visitors attended her ninety-ninth birthday celebration. She tried to shake the hand of every person who came by. Her eyes always lit up for the children, and she would make faces and laugh with them. Many articles about the "princess" remarked on her extraordinary memory, her still-black hair, and her corncob pipe.

For Kilsoquah's one-hundredth birthday in 1910, Dr. Koontz organized an even bigger celebration. Kilsoquah arrived in a large automobile with Dr. Koontz and his wife. The Indiana National Guard performed marching drills and fired gun salutes. A judge read the Declaration of Independence and gave a speech about Kilsoquah's grandfather, Chief Little Turtle, saying that he was one of the nation's greatest early statesmen.

Kilsoquah also made a speech at her birthday celebration. With her son translating, she said, "Marvelous are the changes I have seen; great are the improvements of the years. . . . Only the maker of the bronze man and the white man could give us the old canal, then the railroad, . . . and now the automobile. Yes, the Great Spirit of my forefathers has [created] and [done] well."

Remarkably, Kilsoquah would live five more years. Although her health was declining and she could no longer walk on her own, the last three years of her life were particularly happy due to an amazing turn of events. In 1902, when Kilsoquah was 102, she was reunited with her long-lost daughter, Mary. Mary, looking for help with an unrelated matter, had written a letter to Dr. Koontz, Kilsoquah's doctor. He wrote back, telling Mary that her mother was still living in Roanoke. Elated, Mary hurried to Indiana for a joyous visit with her mother and brother after a decades-long separation. The reunion made all the local newspapers. After that, Mary made frequent visits to Roanoke until Kilsoquah's death in 1905.

Kilsoquah's mind remained sharp until the end. She died peacefully at age 105 and was buried in Glenwood Cemetery, next to her husband, Anthony Revarre. Son Tony moved to Oklahoma to live with his sister. The news of the death of "Princess Kilsoquah," the last Miami Indian in the state, was reported with sadness as the end of an era in Indiana.

Hoosiers never forgot Kilsoquah. Shortly after her death, a state recreation area in Huntington was named for her, and many years later, a historical marker was erected near her grave.

Today, about five hundred registered members of the Miami tribe live in Indiana. They remember and honor Tacumwah, Cates Richardville, Kilsoquah, and many other strong Miami women, reminding us all of their contributions to Indiana history.

Two-story log cabin, built around 1826, where Marie Bailly (1783–1866) lived out her later years. The building, for a time used as a chapel by Marie's descendants, still stands at the Joseph Bailly Homestead, a National Historic Landmark. —Courtesy Calumet Regional Archives

2

MARIE BAILLY

First Settler in Northwest Indiana

Marie LeFevre (la-FEV), later Marie Bailly, lived in two worlds—white and Indian. She was born in 1783 in a land where the native Ottawa Indians and French immigrants lived together. Marie's birthplace was located in what eventually became southeastern Michigan, but at the time it was a sparsely settled U.S. territory—part of the American frontier. Before that, it had been British land, and before that, French, which is why so many of the white settlers in the area were French. Marie's father, Gasçon LeFevre, was a French fur trader, and her mother, Mary, was half French and half Ottawa Indian.

Gasçon LeFevre was well educated and very religious. He taught Marie to read and write in French, and he educated her about the Catholic religion. The family lived in a big white house, designed in the French style, in the newly founded town of Monroe, on Lake Erie, in what is now Michigan. The LeFevres often entertained visitors, as Gasçon was an important man in Monroe.

In 1790, when Marie was seven years old, her father got sick and died. Although Madame LeFevre, Marie, and Marie's little sister Angelique were very sad, they had a nice house, money, and many friends in Monroe, so they thought they'd be all right. Unfortunately, they would learn otherwise when Gasçon's relatives in France heard about his death. They traveled to the LeFevre home and told Mary that she and her girls had to leave. Calling her and her children "half-breeds," a disparaging term meaning part Indian and part white, they said Madame LeFevre could not keep her husband's house or his money because she was Indian—Native Americans had no legal property rights. So Mary had to take her girls away, leaving nearly all of the family's belongings behind.

Madame LeFevre took Marie and Angelique to the Ottawa Indian village at L'Arbre Croche (now Harbor Springs, Michigan) on Lake Michigan, where her relatives lived. The Ottawa welcomed the family, giving them a place to stay and inviting them to be part of the tribal community.

The Ottawa village was very different from Monroe. The whole village lived like one big family. The homes were big, two-story buildings made of logs, called longhouses, each of which housed perhaps a dozen or more families. The longhouses faced an open area where there was always a big campfire burning. Each family had its own sleeping spaces, but everyone shared the cooking and eating areas. Other rooms stored food, garden tools, and other items. The things in the storerooms belonged to the entire village.

The Ottawa were farmers, growing crops of corn, potatoes, beans, and squash. In the winter, the villagers went south to the land of the Potawatomi (in future Indiana) to hunt game until the planting season arrived. The Potawatomi did not mind sharing their hunting grounds because to Native Americans, the land belonged to everyone. In the spring, the Ottawa returned to their villages and settled in to plant their crops. The women handled most of the farm work, while the men provided the village with meat and fish. When they weren't in the fields, the women often sat together, sewing or making baskets as they chatted among themselves. The little children usually stayed with the women, while the older children ran around outside playing games. Adults looked after all the children in the village, not just their own.

Marie's mother had grown up as an Indian, so she was happy living in the Ottawa village. But at first, Marie, whose Ottawa name was Tou-se-qua, did not like living as an Indian. Over the years, however, as she grew up, she absorbed the Ottawa culture, forgetting how to read and write and even how to speak French. Nevertheless, she did not forget her father's Catholic teachings, and she wished to return to that faith when she became a wife. She told her mother that when she grew up, she wanted to marry a French gentleman and live in the white world.

In 1796, when Marie was thirteen, a half- French, half-Ottawa man named Gasçon de La Vigne (VEEN-ya) came to Marie's village looking for a wife. He had a house and property, and he was part French—exactly what Mary LeFevre thought her daughter wanted—so Mary gave Marie to La Vigne as his wife. Marie went with her fiancé to his village to the north, near what is now Mackinaw City, Michigan, where they were married, and she moved into her new husband's house. In time, the couple had two daughters, Agatha and Mary Therese (who went by her middle name).

But La Vigne (whose Ottawa name was Kougowma) was more Indian than European. He was a medicine man of the village, and he followed the spiritual practices of an occult subgroup of Ottawa. His strange rituals, casting spells and putting curses on people, made Marie, who remained faithful to her early upbringing as a Catholic, very uncomfortable—these practices seemed wrong to her.

By Ottawa law, if a girl was married against her wishes, she could divorce the man when she reached maturity. To do so, she had to prepare enough food and clothing for the man for a year. Marie did that, then she took her daughters back to her family's Ottawa village.

Marie supported her children by making crafts, such as fancy embroidery and baskets made of porcupine quills, selling them in the nearby army trading post on Mackinac Island. She was known as much for her beauty as for her excellent work—with her fair skin and thick dark hair, people called her "the Lily of the Lake."

On one trip to Mackinac Island with her daughters, Marie met her second husband. As she stepped out of her canoe, a prominent French Canadian fur trader named Joseph Bailly approached her. A friend of his had pointed her out to him. Joseph told Marie that he knew her name and that he had heard good things about her. That very day, he asked her to be his wife.

Joseph Bailly de Messein was born near Montreal, Canada, in 1774. At age eighteen, he became a fur trader, setting up a trading post in what is now Michigan. By the time he met Marie in 1810, he owned several posts throughout the area. Joseph had three young children from a previous marriage to an Ottawa woman, though they did not live with him.

When Joseph, a Catholic, agreed to adopt her two daughters, aged thirteen and two, Marie consented to marry him. That same evening, Joseph took Marie and her girls to his big house and introduced Marie to the servants as Madame Bailly. From then on, Marie would live in the white world again.

Joseph's business continued to grow. He opened several new trading posts, including two in what would become, in 1816, the state of Indiana. In Mackinac in 1811, Marie gave birth to a daughter, Esther. Two years later, another girl, Rose, was born to the Baillys. In the meantime, the War of 1812 had broken out. Joseph, being from Canada, a British possession, supported the British against the Americans. At first, the war—mostly a fight over national territorial boundries—did not affect the Bailly family. But in January 1813, Joseph was recruited into the Canadian militia. Soon afterward, he led a band of Native Americans in several battles against U.S. troops.

In January 1814, Joseph was arrested as a spy by American soldiers and taken to prison at Fort Detroit, where he remained for three months. He then returned to Mackinac Island and stayed there with his family until after the war ended. In July 1815, the Americans came to take over Mackinac, which was located in territory they had won in the war. Joseph, as a British supporter, was sent back to Canada along with his wife and children. In order to return to Mackinac, Joseph applied for permission to trade in the United States again. The permission was granted in 1817, and the Baillys moved back to Mackinac, where Joseph reestablished his fur business. Soon afterward, Joseph became an American citizen.

Unfortunately, Joseph's wartime experience left him in a weakened condition, although he was still able to work. He taught Marie how to run the trading post, and she managed the business whenever Joseph was ill or when he was away on business. She also had to care for her growing family. Marie and Joseph's third daughter, Eleanor, had arrived in 1815, and in 1817 a boy, Robert, was born. Their fifth and final child, a girl named Josephine Hortense (who went by her middle name), came along two years later.

In 1822 Joseph decided to move his large family to Indiana. All of the younger children went with them, including Therese, Marie's fourteen-year-old daughter from her marriage to Gasçon de La Vigne. Her eldest daughter, Agatha, remained in Mackinac with her husband, Edward Biddle, whom she had married in 1819.

Joseph had chosen a spot near today's Porter, Indiana, where the Calamick (now Calumet) River flowed into Lake Michigan. There were no roads then, but two major trails passed by the place they chose—the Old Sauk Trail, which went from Fort Detroit to Fort Dearborn (Chicago), and the Lake Shore Trail, which skirted the edge of Lake Michigan. Virtually all travelers between Chicago and Detroit, both white and Indian, would pass by their home and trading post. The Bailly property was the first white homestead in Porter County, near the Indiana Dunes, and the trading post would be the only store for miles.

For the family's home, Joseph and his workers built a small log cabin in a grassy spot by a stream. But the cabin didn't stay there. One rainy night, while Joseph was away on a trading trip, Marie woke up to find water all over the floor. She called to the workers to get Joseph's rowboat, and they helped her and the children across the water to the top of a hill. Marie made tents from some blankets, and everyone stayed dry enough to get through the night.

In the morning, Marie took the rowboat back to the flooded house and found that the water was up to her neck. She gathered some food and cooking pots, returned to the hill, and built a campfire. It was good that Marie knew how to live as an Indian—she kept her family comfortable in their makeshift shelter for many days.

When the water went down, Marie told the workers to take the cabin apart, carry the logs to the top of the hill, and put it back together on higher ground. When Joseph got home, Marie jokingly told him that during the flood, the cabin had floated up to the top of the hill. For years afterward, he enjoyed telling that story to visitors.

Near the cabin, the Baillys built a two-story kitchen building, or cookhouse; it was not unusual in those days to do the cooking in a separate structure. The upper floor may have been the sleeping quarters for the family's two servants. Once settled in their home, the Baillys started on the trading post, near the house along the trails. They built a log structure for the store and another nearby for storing the trade goods, such as blankets, tools, and guns. The Baillys, who were fair and honest dealers, soon developed trust with the Potawatomi, Ottawa, and other Indians they traded with.

The Bailly children were all brought up Catholic and all were well educated. The younger ones attended a Baptist mission school near South Bend, while the older ones were sent to Catholic boarding schools in Canada and in Detroit. At school they learned to speak English, French, and Latin in addition to the Indian languages, Ottawa and Potawatomi, they had learned at home. At the homestead, the Bailly children often played with the Ottawa children whose families camped nearby.

Interestingly, though she lived in the white world with her white husband and practiced European Catholism, and though her children were educated in white schools and dressed in Euroamerican clothes, Marie herself held on to many of her Ottawa ways. She wore Indian-style clothing, and she spoke no English and very little French, relying on her multilingual children to translate when she did business with white Americans and Canadians.

At the homestead on long winter nights, Joseph invited the local Indians to come to the house and sit by the fireplace, where he would read them stories from the Bible. The Bailly daughters translated the stories into Potawatomi or Ottawa. Night after night the Indians came to listen.

A musical family, the Baillys had in their home a guitar, a violin, and later even a piano—an unusual item on the frontier. The children learned to play these instruments. When visitors came, the family gathered to play and sing for them.

Sometimes one of the traveling priests who rode through frontier settlements also stopped at the Bailly home. These were very special occasions for the devout family. They would hold church services in their dining room and invite their Indian neighbors to come listen, with the Bailly daughters translating the priest's words, spoken in Latin.

After a few years, other white families came to settle around the Calumet River. Occasionally, conflicts arose between the settlers and the Native Americans who lived or hunted in the area. According to Bailly family lore, Marie, as a member of both societies, once prevented such a conflict from turning violent.

One day an Ottawa woman sent two of her daughters to buy some potatoes from a family of settlers. As the girls passed the farm, they encountered two white boys working in the fields. The boys began teasing the girls, and when the frightened lasses tried to run away, the boys chased after them, grabbed them, and roughly tried to kiss them. Fortunately, the girls were able to get away before the boys could do further harm to them.

While playing with the Ottawa children in their nearby camp, the Bailly children heard about the incident and told Marie and Joseph about it. They said they had also heard that the Ottawa were planning take revenge and attack the settlers. Joseph went to talk with the Ottawa leaders, promising to send the offending boys away. He left thinking that the trouble was over. Marie, however, was not convinced that the Ottawa could be persuaded so easily. She sent her children to play at the Ottawa camp each day and report to her about what they saw. She knew the Ottawa people would not harm the children, but if they decided to make war, all the settlers would be killed. Three days later, the children described activities that told Marie they were preparing for war.

Marie went with Joseph to talk to the Ottawa leaders again. Standing by their big campfire, she began to pray loudly to the

Christian God in the Ottawa language. The Ottawa recognized the prayers from the times they had visited the Bailly home to listen to Bible stories. Marie prayed all night. When morning came, the Ottawa packed up their camp and boarded their canoes, saying they would not be coming back to the Calumet.

In 1827 tragedy struck the Bailly family when Joseph and Marie's only son, Robert, died of typhoid at age ten. Joseph buried him on the north side of the Bailly property and erected a large white cross near the grave. This area would become the Bailly family cemetery, where many family members would be buried upon their deaths. Joseph also built a small log chapel nearby, where the family would go to worship each Sunday.

By the early 1830s, the fur-trade business had dramatically declined, so Joseph decided to invest in a new enterprise with better prospects. He built an inn, or tavern, about three-quarters of a mile north of their home along a newly built stagecoach road, where weary travelers would easily find it. At the Bailly Tavern, they could get a good meal and a bed for a reasonable price. It soon became a very busy place.

The Bailly homestead continued to grow. By the time they opened the inn, the property had several storehouses and bunkhouses as well as horse stables. In 1830 Marie's daughter Therese married Peter Nadeau. The couple lived on the Bailly homestead, where they helped run the family businesses, and eventually they had four children. Four years after Therese's wedding, Esther Bailly married John H. Whistler and moved to the emerging city of Chicago.

As more settlers moved into northwest Indiana, Joseph Bailly dreamed of expanding. In 1833 he purchased a large parcel of land—some 2,000 acres—about a mile west of their homestead, where he planned to build a town. The chosen site was near Lake Michigan, and Joseph believed his town could be a port for ships. He made a plat map and named his planned settlement Town Bailly (better known as Baillytown). He marked off the streets, which he named after his children.

Joseph also started to build a large new house for his family, as well as some other structures on the homestead. But before the house was finished, he got very sick. He was moved to a warm and quiet spot to recover, but he never did. On December 21, 1835, Joseph Bailly died. He was buried near Robert in the family cemetery.

Needless to say, Marie grieved, but she carried on. Upon Joseph's death, daughter Esther returned to the homestead with her husband and children, moving into the newly built big house. Marie, who preferred cozier quarters, moved into the two-story former cookhouse. The original cabin was turned into a chapel for the family and their white and Indian neighbors. With the help of her children and her sons-in-law, Marie took over the operation of Joseph's store and inn. Joseph's heirs also attempted to keep Baillytown going, hoping to fulfill Joseph's dream, but virtually no one bought a lot there.

Unfortunately, it was not long before Marie lost the assistance of her daughters and their spouses. In 1839, during the mass relocation of the Potawatomi and other tribes from Indiana, Therese, Peter, and their children moved to the Indian reservation in Kansas. Two years later, Rose Bailly married Francis Howe and moved to Chicago. That same year, Eleanor Bailly moved to the Terre Haute area to become a nun. She joined the Sisters of Providence and became a special associate of Mother Théodore Guérin, whom we will meet later in this book. When Mother Théodore died, Eleanor, now called Sister Mary Cecilia, became the Mother Superior of the Sisters of Providence.

The year after Rose and Eleanor left, 1842, Esther Bailly Whistler died at the homestead while giving birth to her fifth child. John Whistler took his children and moved out of the state. After Esther's death, Rose and her husband, Francis, came back to the homestead to help Marie, though they still had a home in Chicago and their children were all born there. Francis managed the homestead very well. He built a sawmill and harvested timber from the property, selling lumber to the railroad that was being built through Porter County, as well as to settlers in the area.

The next seven years were quiet ones. When Rose and her family were in Chicago, Marie had only her youngest daughter, Hortense, with her at the homestead. Then, in 1849, Hortense married Joel Wicker and she, too, moved to Chicago. At that point, rather than stay in Indiana all alone, Marie decided to move to the city to be near her daughters.

The Bailly family's woes were not yet over, however. In 1850, a deadly cholera epidemic struck Chicago. Rose was expecting her fifth child when her husband, Francis Howe, and three of the couple's children died of the disease. After the baby was born, Rose, her two children, and Marie returned to the Indiana homestead. Rose and her two young daughters lived in the big house while Marie returned to the two-story log building nearby, where she would live for the remainder of her life. Hortense's husband, Joel Wicker, took over the main management of the property for several years. Like his brother-in-law, he was very successful, expanding the sawmill and lumber business as more and more settlers—primarily Swedish immigrants—came to Porter County. Over time, the Baillytown lots were sold to these settlers, while the homestead and cemetery remained in the Bailly family.

Marie was to witness one more untimely death before her own life was over. In 1855 Hortense Bailly Wicker, like her sister before her, died in childbirth. After that, only Rose and her two little girls remained with Marie at the homestead.

Marie Bailly died on September 15, 1866, at age eighty-three. She was laid to rest beside her husband in the family cemetery. After Marie's death, daughter Rose managed the homestead property until she passed away in 1891, then it went to her daughter Frances, who never married. After Frances died in 1917, the Bailly homestead was donated to the School Sisters of Notre Dame of the Lake, who used it as a retreat for some years. Eventually, the property was designated a National Historic Landmark, and in 1971 it was acquired by the National Park Service, which now preserves it as part of the Indiana Dunes National Lakeshore.

Marie LeFevre Bailly will be remembered for the many things she was: an intrepid pioneer of early Indiana; a devoted wife, mother, and Catholic; the matriarch of a large, successful family; and a businesswoman in her own right. Not least of all, as the child of a French father and an Ottawa mother, Marie Bailly was a lifelong friend to whites and Indians alike.

Portrait of Mother Théodore Guérin (1798–1852). The date of the painting and the artist are unknown. —Courtesy Sisters of Providence

MOTHER THÉODORE GUÉRIN

Frontier Educator and Catholic Saint

When Anne-Thérèse (ahn teh-REZ) Guérin (GAIR-in) was a little girl in Brittany, France, she loved to stand on the rocks by the Atlantic Ocean, looking out at the gray waves, feeling the cool wind in her face, and thinking about the big world out there. Even at a young age, Anne-Thérèse knew she wanted two things: to travel to faraway places and to devote her life to the Catholic Church. By the end of her life, the extraordinarily strong-willed Anne-Thérèse Guérin would accomplish both goals, traveling across that big cold ocean three times and becoming not just a nun, but a Mother Superior. Most remarkably, 150 years after her 1856 death, Mother Théodore Guérin was canonized (declared a saint) by the pope as Saint Theodora.

What had Mother Théodore done to merit this transcendent honor? As a missionary in 1840, she led a group of brave sisters through the American wilderness to the young state of Indiana to start schools for frontier children. Thanks to Mother Théodore's iron-willed determination, the sisters overcame great obstacles—including conflicts with church leaders—to open numerous schools, two orphanages, several health clinics, and even a college. Years after her death, the Catholic Church recognized two miracles of healing attributed to her, and she was canonized in 2006.

Anne-Thérèse Guérin was born in the small town of Étables, in the Brittany region of northwestern France, on October 2, 1798. At that time, the country was all torn up from the French Revolution, a civil war that had begun nine years earlier. Under King Louis XVI, many working people were starving while the wealthy enjoyed an abundant life, and most workers believed that a drastic change in leadership was needed. Thus the French people were divided between those who supported the king and those who wanted democracy, and mass violence erupted. In 1793 the rebels executed the king and queen, launching a year-long "Reign of Terror." It was a scary time for everyone, particularly for Catholics, who were persecuted by the rebels because they felt that the church had too much power.

Anne-Thérèse's father, Laurent Guérin, was an officer in the French Navy, so while Anne-Thérèse was growing up, he was usually away from home. When Anne-Thérèse was two years old, her older brother, Jean-Laurent, died when the family's house caught fire. Their mother, Isabelle, was so sad she could barely take care of Anne-Thérèse or herself. A few years later, however, when Anne-Thérèse was five, a happy event occurred when her little sister, Marie-Jeanne, was born.

Due to the chaos during and after the revolution, many schools were closed down, so Isabelle taught her girls to read and write using the family's few books, which were mostly religious texts. For a short time, when she was nine, Anne-Thérèse attended a local school that had opened, but she did not like it and often skipped classes. "As soon as I understood that it was wrong to play hookey, I was careful not to [do it] again," she recalled.

Anne-Thérèse also learned much from her cousin, a seminary student who had moved in with the Guérins to hide from the wrath of the rebels. He taught Anne-Thérèse about the church, world history, and other subjects. The young girl was so devoted to her religion that she even had her own little altar in her room, where she prayed to the Virgin Mary. At age ten, Anne-Thérèse took her First

Communion, at which time she told the priest that she intended to become a nun and dedicate her life to God.

When Anne-Thérèse was eleven, a little brother, named Laurent after his father, was born. Tragically, when he was only four years old, Laurent, like his brother before him, died in a fire. Little did the grieving family know that their misfortune had only begun. By this time, Anne-Thérèse's father was serving under General Napoleon Bonaparte, who had become France's emperor a few years after the revolution. In April 1814, Napoleon lost a major battle and was forced out of office. The navy was disbanded, and Monsieur Guérin left for home. He was making his way home through the French countryside when, in June 1814, a gang of bandits attacked him in the woods, robbed him, and killed him.

Upon hearing of her husband's death, only six months after losing her second child, Isabelle Guérin was overcome with grief. She became an invalid, seldom getting out of bed, leaving Anne-Thérèse, only fifteen years old, to take over the care of the family. The girl also had to find work, since her father's death meant the family had no income. For several years, Anne-Thérèse worked as a seamstress to support her mother and sister.

When she turned twenty, Anne-Thérèse felt it was time to start her own life, and she told her mother of her desire to become a nun. Although Madame Guérin was still unwell, Anne-Thérèse thought that her sister, Marie-Jeanne, now fifteen, was old enough to take care of herself and their mother. But Madame Guérin said she could not bear to see Anne-Thérèse go. Sympathetic to her mother's suffering, Anne-Thérèse agreed to stay at home, but over the next few years she asked her mother again and again for permission to join a convent. Finally, when Anne-Thérèse was twenty-five, Isabelle realized that she was keeping her daughter from her true calling and told Anne-Thérèse that she could go. "I can no longer refuse God the sacrifice he is asking of me," she said to her daughter.

Anne-Thérèse joined the Sisters of Providence, a new congregation of nuns in Ruillé-sur-Loir, some 300 kilometers (about 200 miles) from her home. Upon entering the congregation, she followed the traditional practice of taking a new name to represent her new life as a sister. The names came from the Roman Catholic saints. Choosing Saint Théodore, Anne-Thérèse Guérin became Sister Saint Théodore Guérin.

The Sisters of Providence, headed by Mother Mary Lacor, decided to send Sister Théodore to teach school in a nearby town, but before she was able to leave, Théodore became seriously ill with smallpox. Although smallpox was often fatal, Sister Théodore recovered. Unfortunately, the medicine the doctor had treated her with ruined her digestive system, and Sister Théodore could never again eat anything but bland soups, juices, and watery oatmeal.

Sister Théodore taught for a few years in the schools run by the Sisters of Providence. She became known as a teacher who could help students with behavior problems. Maybe she understood these kids because she had been a strong-willed child herself, and because she had known suffering, which often led to a troubled mind and misbehavior.

In 1826, Sister Théodore's third year as a nun, Mother Mary sent her to teach at a recently opened girls' school in an impoverished neighborhood in the war-ravaged town of Rennes (ren). Everyone said the students at that school were so wild that no one could teach them. On the first day, the girls paid no attention to Sister Théodore. When she told the students that they must cooperate with her for their own good—that she was there to help them—they shouted and laughed. All Sister Théodore could do was remain calm. She knew that her job would require all the patience she had.

The next day was no better. After a little while of sitting still, the girls could not contain themselves. They jumped up and began dancing around the room. Sister Théodore watched silently until the girls settled down of their own accord and waited for their teacher's reaction. With all eyes on her, Sister Théodore quietly picked up the stick that was used to whip the children. The girls held their breath. Who would the teacher beat first? To their surprise, she instead broke the stick into little pieces and dropped them into the wastebasket. Then she reached into her pocket and pulled out a little paper ticket. She explained that the girls who behaved would be rewarded with these tickets, which they could exchange for treats or prizes. Over the next few months, the class's behavior gradually improved.

As the children became more serious and studious, the whole neighborhood seemed to blossom. One sister remarked that the transformation was thanks to "the zeal, the enlightened piety, and the outstanding qualities" of Sister Théodore.

Sister Théodore taught her students basic reading and writing as well as prayers and catechism (Christian teachings). The girls also learned knitting, sewing, and other skills that would allow them to earn a living. Soon, because she was so effective, Sister Théodore was put in charge of eight schools in Rennes. Before long, the people of Rennes came to love and respect Sister Théodore. As one observer noted, "their admiration for her virtues and talents, and their confidence in her were such as might be expected from their having seen the good she effected where everything seemed hopeless and almost impossible."

In spite of her remarkable success, Sister Théodore unwittingly got into trouble while she was in Rennes. For some time, Mother Mary had been concerned that the elderly priest who handled the congregation's money was putting the sisters into serious debt. Frustrated, she asked the bishop to have the priest turn the finances over to her, and her request was granted. This turn of events threw the old priest into a deep depression. Strangely, rumors began to circulate that Sister Théodore had been sympathizing with the priest and was criticizing the bishop's decision. Mother Mary heard the rumors and became angry with Sister Théodore. Théodore firmly denied the accusation, but when Mother Mary sent her on a new mission, far away from Rennes, in 1834, some felt that she had done it to punish Sister Théodore.

Leaving Rennes after eight happy and productive years deeply saddened not only Sister Théodore herself but also her students and the entire community. Yet she had no choice but to obey her superior. She was sent to a tiny, poor rural village called Soulaines to teach school and minister to the sick there. Although she was unhappy at first, she enjoyed the peace and quiet of the little village. Embracing her new duties, she began working with a local doctor in order to learn about treatments and medicines. Later on, she would be glad that she learned these things. It was not long before the needy people of Soulaines turned to Sister Théodore whenever they needed help of any kind.

In 1839, after five years in Soulaines, Sister Théodore was stunned when Mother Mary told her something that would change her life. The Mother Superior explained that she had received a letter from Bishop Simon Bruté of Vincennes, Indiana, asking for five sisters to come to America and start a school. America! The New World. Mother Mary said she wanted one of those sisters to be Théodore.

Although Sister Théodore thought she would love to go to America, at age forty-one and in poor health, she thought she was too old and sickly for such a challenging job. But Mother Mary insisted that Sister Théodore was the only one with the qualities needed to lead the mission. She would not send a group of sisters to Indiana without her. Once again, Théodore obeyed what she considered a calling from God and agreed to go to Indiana.

Going from France to Indiana was a long, hard journey in those days. In July 1840, after bidding a tearful final goodbye to the place and people they loved, knowing they would likely never return to France, Sister Théodore and her four companions traveled to Le Havre, where they boarded an American merchant ship and set sail across the Atlantic.

The trip was rough, and the boat often rocked violently on the waves, making the sisters so seasick they could not eat. But when, after seven weeks, New York Harbor finally came into view, all discomfort was forgotten. In a letter she wrote onboard, Sister Théodore expressed her feelings upon seeing the American shore for the first time: "Rejoice, my Mother and my very dear Sisters, rejoice! [God] has guided your daughters over the immense abyss of the sea. . . . How fast my heart is beating!"

Landing in New York, after nearly two months on the ship, the sisters may have thought that the worst part of their trip was over, but in fact it still lay before them. In New York, they learned that the bishop who asked for them, Simon Bruté, had died. They expected that the Bishop of Vincennes, Monsignor de la Hailandière (hi-ond-YAIR), would have sent someone to meet them and lead them to Indiana, but they received no word from him. Some people from the ship, however, came to the rescue of the sisters, who spoke no English, contacting the bishop of New York, who found them lodging in the area.

After five days in New York, the sisters received word from the Bishop of Vincennes. They were told to proceed by train to Philadelphia, where someone would meet them. When the sisters arrived in that city, they were taken to meet the local bishop, who treated them with utmost consideration. In Philadelphia they learned that a French Canadian priest who was also headed to Vincennes, Father William Chartier, would accompany them the rest of the way.

The little group took a train to Baltimore, then to Frederick, Maryland, where they boarded a riverboat that took them down the Ohio River to Cincinnati. The boat trip took four days. They slept on thin, dirty mattresses on the floor, in a cabin crowded with women and children, all of whom spoke only English, which the sisters did not understand. In Cincinnati, the sisters began to see the poverty of the frontier. From there they took another steamboat to Madison, Indiana, where they hoped to finally meet their bishop, Monsignor de la Hailandière.

The sisters arrived in Madison to find that the bishop was not there. They stayed at a small inn and waited for several days. Finally Bishop de la Hailandière appeared in Madison for a brief visit. He told the sisters that he was still traveling and that they should go on to Vincennes and wait for him there. He also told them that the new boarding school, where the sisters were to teach, would not be built in Vincennes. Instead, the sisters would be living and working many miles away, in the little village of St. Mary-of-the-Woods, near Terre Haute. Sister Théodore was surprised and worried to hear this, as nothing was turning out as she expected. Instead of teaching in a growing town, she and her fellow nuns would be in an isolated village in the woods. Where would their students come from? Nevertheless, she was not afraid, trusting that the Lord was guiding her.

Following the bishop's instructions, the sisters boarded another steamboat and traveled to Evansville, Indiana; from there, they took a stagecoach to Vincennes. The trip there was a rough ride on a dirt road. Upon their arrival at Vincennes, the sisters went to the unfinished cathedral, meant to be the head church for all of Indiana. Sister Théodore cried when she saw how poor it looked—bricks falling out, broken windows, and a wooden steeple that was already rotting.

When Bishop de la Hailandière returned, the sisters went to his home to receive instructions. While there, they met the pastor at St. Mary-of-the-Woods, Father Buteaux, who would accompany them to their new home. The five nuns and the priest, who was also French, boarded another stagecoach to St. Mary-of-the-Woods, riding along an even bumpier road. When they arrived, after dark, Father Buteaux led the sisters through the woods until they came to a farmhouse. It was the home of a local family, where the sisters would be staying until their convent was finished. Not far from the house was a small log cabin with no roof—this was the chapel. It was also, they learned, Father Buteaux's living quarters. The original church and rectory had recently burned down. Their new lives, the nuns now knew, would be simple and poor, but they gave thanks that their long journey was over.

The main house belonged to a family named Thralls. The sisters would live in their attic until their new place could be finished in the spring. Upon meeting the Thralls family, Sister Théodore and her companions were introduced to four other women, postulants (candidates to be nuns) who wanted to join the congregation. The Sisters of Providence would now have nine members. Three of the postulants were American and one was French. The Americans would teach the French sisters English, to prepare them for teaching American children.

When the sisters climbed up to the attic to sleep that first night, they saw that their beds were sacks stuffed with straw arranged on the floor. The roof had leaks that let in rain and snow and wind, and the attic received little heat from the fireplace downstairs. Their kitchen, they learned, would be a shed. They would also have one larger room they could use as a communal space.

The next morning, Sister Théodore and her group went to look at the convent in progress. It was a two-story brick building nestled deep in the woods. It would be very nice, but in the meantime, they were facing a long, cold winter.

A short time later, Sister Théodore found out that the Thralls family had another house nearby, where they were willing to move. This gave her an idea. When Bishop de la Hailandière came to visit, Théodore explained to him that the sisters' current quarters were so cramped, they were hardly able to get anything done. She told him about the Thralls family's other house and asked him if he might buy their current house for the sisters. That way they would have plenty of space, and they could even fix the leaks. When the brick building was finished in the spring, it could be used for a church and school instead of living quarters. At first the bishop was hesitant, but he said he'd think about it. As he was leaving, the bishop told the sisters to call Sister Théodore "Mother" Théodore, as a sign of her leadership. From then on, she was addressed as Mother. A few days later, the bishop told the sisters that he had paid Mr. Thralls and the house was theirs.

Mother Théodore became very ill over the winter, but she slowly recovered. When spring finally came, the sisters planted a garden with lots of vegetables. They also had chickens, a few pigs, and a milk cow. Their little farm needed to produce enough food to feed themselves and their students and get them through the next winter. A barn was built to shelter the livestock and store grain.

When the brick building was completed, the sisters sent out letters to settlers in the area saying that their girls' school would open in July. On July 2, 1841, St. Mary's Institute opened with nineteen paying students. Interestingly, most of the girls were Protestant, as Catholic families tended to be too poor to pay for private boarding school for their daughters. But the Sisters of Providence did not mind—their school was open to any child. Later, when the congregation could afford it, the school admitted nonpaying students as well.

During the course of the first year, a few of the original postulants left the congregation, but many other new ones joined, including one Eleanor Bailly, daughter of early Indiana settlers Joseph and Marie Bailly, whom we met in the second chapter of this book. She became Sister Mary Cecilia.

When fall came, Mother Théodore traveled to Vincennes for the dedication of the new cathedral there. She was delighted to see that the dilapidated shack she had seen months before had been transformed into a beautiful, though simple, building.

The school and convent at St. Mary-of-the-Woods was also blossoming. Additions were built onto the house, the farm was productive, and more students enrolled in the school. Nevertheless, the sisters would have their ups and downs. One sister left the congregation to start her own school in Terre Haute, and the new school drew students away from St. Mary's, leaving the Sisters of Providence with only ten students, all nonpaying. Lack of money continued to be a problem. But Mother Théodore and her sisters bore all burdens cheerfully.

Over the next several years, priests at two other towns asked Théodore to send sisters to start schools, which she did. Meanwhile at St. Mary's, the sisters started a free day school for the poor children who lived near their village. Open to both boys and girls, the school offered classes after regular school hours, teaching skills such as woodworking, cooking, and sewing, in addition to reading and writing.

In the fall of 1842, the congregation had a terrible setback. After harvesting all their wheat and corn, the sisters stored it in their barn. One night, the barn caught fire and burned to the ground, along with all the grain. Now they would not have enough food for themselves and the children through the winter.

Fortunately, when word of the disaster reached the sisters' supporters in America and in France, including Bishop de la Hailandière and Mother Mary, they sent the sisters donations of money and goods, saving the congregation from starving. They even had enough left over to build a new barn. In other good news, later that fall, St. Mary's received a permanent chaplain, an intelligent and agreeable young priest, originally from France, named Father Corbe.

The sisters made it through the winter, but financial problems continued to plague the congregation at St. Mary's. Bishop de la Hailandière told them he could no longer afford to help them as he had been because his own needs in Vincennes were too great. Mother Théodore, who wished to expand her mission, decided to take a trip to France to raise money, as well as to seek advice from Mother Mary. She and a companion, Sister Mary Cecilia (Eleanor Bailly), left for Europe in April 1843. The voyage was largely uneventful.

In France, the sisters visited many old friends and superiors, including Mother Mary, a particularly joyous reunion for Théodore. The sisters were not very successful, however, in raising funds. Mother Théodore was ready to give up when something wonderful happened. They had traveled to Paris, where someone suggested they approach the queen of France. The queen, a religious woman, received the sisters and listened to them with great interest. She promised to give them enough money for their passage home and additional funds as well.

While the sisters would have liked to stay longer in France, where they might raise more money, troubling letters from St. Mary's convinced Mother Théodore that they needed to return to Indiana as soon as possible. The congregation was in turmoil over Bishop de la Hailandière's increasingly overbearing and unpredictable behavior. Théodore's friends in France promised to continue raising money for the congregation after she left.

As soon as possible, Mother Théodore and Sister Cecilia, along with two new French postulants, sailed across the Atlantic Ocean again. It was a rough trip—they ran into several fierce storms, and at one point the ship nearly capsized. The passengers were deeply grateful when they landed in New Orleans.

Shortly after the nuns' arrival in New Orleans, Mother Théodore became very sick. She told Sister Cecilia to go on to Indiana without her, taking the money they'd collected in France home to the Sisters of Providence, because they needed it right away. One of the postulants accompanied Sister Cecilia back to St. Mary's while the other remained with Mother Théodore in New Orleans, where they stayed with the Ursuline Sisters through the winter. When spring came, Mother Théodore was feeling strong enough to go on home. She knew from the many letters she had received from St. Mary's, however, that many changes awaited her upon her return, most of them unpleasant.

While Mother Théodore was away, Bishop de la Hailandière had become unbearably domineering and hostile. He told the sisters that he, not Mother Théodore, had authority over their congregation. Among other things, he had forced the the Sisters of Providence to accept some new postulants and had moved several of the older sisters to other communities. He had even held an election for the nuns to choose a new Mother Superior; the sisters made him angry when they voted unanimously for Mother Théodore, even though she had yet to return. The sisters had written to Mother Mary and to several bishops in America and France communicating their dismay at Bishop de la Hailandière's actions. Siding with the sisters, some sent him reprimands, but to no avail.

For his own part, Bishop de la Hailandière was not exactly happy. In fact, he had submitted his resignation to his superiors, but the resignation needed to be approved by the pope in Rome. In the meantime, he was still the Bishop of Vincennes.

Mother Théodore finally reached Indiana in the spring of 1844 and headed straight to Vincennes to talk to the bishop. He was more than unfriendly—in fact, he soon became furious, demanding that

Mother Théodore give him the money she'd collected in France. He accused her of telling lies about him to the French bishops. He insisted on his authority. Mother Théodore remained as calm as she could. Finally, he allowed her to return to St. Mary's.

The Sisters of Providence now had some money, and things went well for months, but the fear of the bishop's wrath remained. He refused to approve the rules for the sisters' order, rules that Mother Théodore was deeply devoted to. He would not allow them to build additions to the school, which was becoming overcrowded. He demanded that the sisters retract the terrible things they had said about him, even though they had said very little. He tried to send their chaplain, Father Corbe, to another town. He wanted to replace Théodore as Mother Superior at St. Mary's and send her away. He threatened to remove the sisters and shut down St. Mary's. None of these things happened, but the sisters were constantly worried.

In April 1847, Mother Théodore went to Vincennes to meet again with Bishop de la Hailandière. It was worse than before. The bishop told her he had already dismissed her from St. Mary's but she continued to defy his orders. When she objected, saying an election must be held, he became enraged. Incredibly, he left the room and locked the door behind him. He kept Théodore in the room for hours, until it was dark outside. The sisters in Vincennes became worried about her and went to the bishop's house to ask him where she was. He calmly opened the door of the locked room and told Mother Théodore she could leave, acting as if nothing was wrong.

The sisters returned to the convent at Vincennes, but later that evening the bishop came over, angrier than ever. He told Théodore that she was no longer the head of the Sisters of Providence, that in fact she was no longer a nun—he released her from her vows. She must go away, he said. She was never to return to St. Mary-of-the-Woods, or even to write letters to the sisters there.

When the stagecoach from Vincennes arrived at St. Mary's without Mother Théodore, the sisters were afraid she was ill again, but Sister Mary Xavier, who had been with Mother Théodore in Vincennes, informed them, through choking tears, of what had happened. The sisters and Father Corbe gathered together and decided that if Théodore did not return, they would all leave St. Mary's. They wrote to the bishop informing him of their decision, even though he had threatened to excommunicate—expel from the Catholic Church—anyone who defied his orders. They also wrote letters to all the church people they knew back in France to tell them what had happened.

In the meantime, in Vincennes, Mother Théodore fell ill again. This was hardly surprising given her fragile health, the fatigue from traveling, and most of all the mental anguish she was suffering from.

Just as the situation looked completely hopeless, Mother Théodore received some fantastic news. The pope had written to Bishop de la Hailandière accepting his resignation. He was no longer a bishop, starting immediately. Father Corbe would be in charge until a new bishop arrived.

The news revived Mother Théodore's spirits, and she began to recover. By mid-June she was back at St. Mary's. The sisters, the students, even the workmen came out to meet her, with much rejoicing. Mother Théodore was home at last, and their darkest days were now behind them.

The new bishop, a Frenchman by birth, was an older man, reputed to be humble and kind. Indeed, Bishop Bazin was very attentive to the Sisters of Providence, helping them start new schools and medical clinics. Sadly, Bishop Bazin took ill a short time later and died the following spring. His replacement, Monsignor de Saint-Palais, who had been Bishop Bazin's chosen successor, was also very supportive of the sisters at St. Mary's. Mother Théodore continued to lead the congregation freely until her death many years later.

In the ensuing years, St. Mary's thrived. They always had plenty to eat, and the congregation continued to grow. More sisters and postulants joined the Sisters of Providence until there were nearly one hundred by 1853, spread throughout the area. The sisters started schools in towns all over Indiana; eventually, a thousand students were enrolled. The sisters also managed two orphanges in Vincennes, and they continued to provide medical care for communities in the area.

Mother Théodore, unfortunately, continued to suffer from frequent bouts of illness. In the spring of 1856, her condition worsened; she took to her bed and spoke very little. The doctor said she had a serious heart condition. On May 11, Father Corbe came to her bedside and gave her the Last Sacraments; three days later he gave her final absolution and recited the prayers for the dying, with many of the sisters present. Then, in the early morning hours of May 14, 1856, she quietly passed away.

Anne-Thérèse Guérin, Mother Théodore, was only fifty-seven when she died, but her legacy would endure. "We shall follow the path she traced out for us. . . . With this prospect before us, even in our tears we are happy," wrote Sister Mary Cecilia of her dear mentor's death. Sister Cecilia, born Eleanor Bailly, would become the new Mother Superior of the Sisters of Providence. The white cross over her grave was inscribed, "I sleep, but my heart watches over this house that I have built."

In 2006, Pope Benedict XVI declared Mother Théodore a saint. Her official name is Saint Theodora Guérin, but the Sisters of Providence refer to her as Saint Mother Théodore because she was very much their spiritual mother. Saint Theodora was the eighth American, and the first person from Indiana, to be canonized as a Roman Catholic saint. Her shrine is located in St. Mary-of-the-Woods, Indiana.

Pen-and-ink portrait of poet Sarah Bolton (1814–93) by John Sartain, circa 1889.

4

SARAH BOLTON

Indiana's Pioneer Poet

Sarah Barrett Bolton's earliest memory was the day her family left their nice home and good friends in Newport, Kentucky, to move to the wilderness of Indiana. It was 1818; Indiana had become a state just two years before.

Future poet Sarah Tittle Barrett was born on December 18, 1814. Her father was Jonathan Barrett, an army colonel from a prominent Kentucky family. Her mother, Esther Pendleton Barrett, came from an even more prominent Virginia family—Esther was the first cousin of President James Madison, who was serving in that office when Sarah was born.

Sarah remembered watching her mother close the door of their house in Newport for the last time. Mrs. Barrett stood on the front step with a baby in her arms, tears running down her face as she said goodbye to friends and neighbors. Little Sarah, the eldest at age three, and her sister, two years younger, stood beside her in mute confusion.

A military band played a lively tune for the colonel's family as they walked down the street to the dock, where a large flatboat waited to take them down the Ohio River to Louisville, Kentucky, where they would meet up with Sarah's father. Colonel Barrett had gone ahead to Indiana several months earlier to buy a farm and build a log house for his family. He then returned to Louisville, staying at the home of his in-laws, James and Esther Pendleton, to await the arrival of his wife and children. It would take Mrs. Barrett and the children two weeks to float the 120 miles down to Louisville. From there Colonel Barrett would lead them on horseback to their new home in southeastern Indiana.

Sarah remembered the flatboat trip, floating "down the beautiful Ohio, through fair days and starry nights," as she described it. The family's beds and trunks were at one end of the boat, and their horses were in stalls at the other end. In the middle was a living space for the family, complete with a cookstove and a table and chairs.

When the boat arrived in Louisville, the family spent a few days visiting with Sarah's grandparents before setting off through the thick woods of Indiana to their new home. There was no road for wagons, so they had to ride horses, bringing only what belongings they could carry on horseback. Sarah, her mother, and the baby rode on one horse, while Colonel Barrett and Sarah's sister rode on another. A third horse carried the family's supplies, including bedding, clothing, bacon, flour, coffee, and tools. It took the Barrett family several days to reach their destination, following the narrow trail through the dense woods and fording the swollen Muscatatuck River to the little town of Vernon; from there, they rode northeast six miles to their new home.

When the family moved into the little cabin Colonel Barrett had built for them, filled with rough-hewn log furniture he had also built, his wife did not complain. But as Mrs. Barrett put supper on the table that night, Sarah saw silent tears falling down her mother's face. Esther had grown up in town and knew little about farming. "But with a true heart and strong hands," Sarah recalled, "she took up her burden and bore it bravely and patiently to the end. . . . I have never known her equal in all that goes to make up a noble character."

The Barrett farm was on Six-Mile Creek, in the southeastern part of the state. While in Indiana, Colonel and Mrs. Barrett had five more children, giving Sarah a total of seven siblings. Everyone worked hard to earn the family's living; even the children helped plow the fields and harvest the crops. In addition to their farm chores, such as milking the cow and feeding the chickens, Sarah and her sisters learned to cook, wash clothes by hand, sew, and spin yarn.

Although Sarah and her siblings had to work hard, their mother took time each night to tell them fairy tales. Their father, too, told them stories, such as the tale of Robin Hood and his band of Merry Men in Sherwood Forest. These stories fed Sarah's imagination with images that later showed up in her writing.

From an early age, Sarah showed the heart of a poet. She loved to take a bucket to Six-Mile Spring, where she watched the water shoot up into the air like a fountain. She often went at night, and years later she remembered seeing the droplets of water shining like pearls in the starlight.

Sarah also recalled a childhood adventure. One afternoon Sarah and the eldest of her younger sisters rode their family horse six miles to their neighbors' house, as they often did, to play with friends. On the way home, the girls wandered off the path to gather wild grapes. Soon they were lost. As darkness fell, they came to the campsite of a Native American family, probably of the Shawnee tribe. Sarah was not afraid of the local Indians, as they were known to be peaceful.

Sarah saw that the mother of this family was sick, lying on a bearskin as her children played around her. The father was preparing a deer he had just killed for their dinner. Sarah approached the father, who understood some English, and told him they were lost. The man said he knew their father and that the colonel was a good man. He added that he knew Mrs. Barrett, too; she had once given his ailing wife a blanket. He gladly agreed to lead the girls back home. Later, when Sarah read stories of vicious Indians attacking white settlers, she knew it was not the whole truth.

In those early days of Indiana, community facilities such as schools and churches were scarce, especially on the frontier. To serve the spiritual needs of isolated farm families like the Barretts, traveling preachers sometimes came riding through. One day, when Sarah was about eight, one of these preachers came to the Barrett farm and told them he would hold a service that Sunday in a nearby grove of maple trees. He was a tall, thin man with long black hair. Eager to hear a sermon, the Barretts invited their neighbors and the people from the town of Vernon to come out to hear the preacher as well.

That Sunday, the Barretts and many of their neighbors gathered in the maple grove to wait for the preacher. He arrived wearing leather leggings, a coonskin cap, an Indian belt, and moccasins. The preacher held his audience spellbound as he spoke with great power about sin, punishment, and the Day of Judgement. His words brought the men, women, and children to tears. Then he left, and they never saw him again.

This sermon made an enormous impression on young Sarah. As she later said, it "took such a hold on my imagination that I could scarcely eat or sleep till I had composed a song" about it. She sang this song over and over to herself when she was alone in the woods. Later, when she learned how to write, she wrote down the words of the song. It was her first poem. This early poem has been lost to history, so we don't know exactly what it said, but religious themes and images appear frequently in Sarah's later poetry.

Just as there were no churches near the Barrett homestead, there were no schools either. Colonel Barrett knew that if he wanted his children to get a good education he'd have to move his family to a town with schools. In 1824, deciding that his children's education was the most important thing, Colonel Barrett sold the farm, even though he had put years of work into building it, and moved his family to Madison, Indiana, about thirty miles south of the farm. It was a big sacrifice, but the colonel was a caring father who put his children first.

When Sarah started school in Madison, she did not know how to read and write. Seeing that the other ten-year-olds were way ahead of her, she was embarrassed. Determined to catch up, she studied hard, and within two months she could read and write just as well as her classmates. She used her new skills to start writing down the rhymes she made up. She found that she adored reading, and she was interested in many subjects. Sarah worked so hard that when she finished elementary school, she was named the smartest girl in her class. The smartest boy was Jesse D. Bright, whom Sarah would meet again later in life, when Jesse was a state legislator and, after that, a U.S. senator.

Upon completing primary school, Sarah entered secondary school, where she studied geography, chemistry, and Latin, among other subjects. Many people thought it was silly for a girl to learn Latin, since in those days only men went to college and became professionals. This attitude made Sarah so self-conscious that she quit her Latin class. But she still wanted to learn as much as she could, and soon she had read every book her school had. One day, a judge and future legislator in Madison named Jeremiah Sullivan, who had heard about Sarah's sharp mind, met with her and told her that she could borrow any books she wanted from his own library. This opened up a whole new world to Sarah, and she was forever grateful for the judge's generosity.

All the time she attended school, Sarah was writing poetry. When she was thirteen years old, she sent a poem to the local newspaper, the *Madison Republican,* and to her delight, the paper printed it. Encouraged, she sent the paper a new poem almost every week. A newspaper in Cincinnati, Ohio, also published some of Sarah's poems. By the age of sixteen, Sarah Barrett was a well-known poet.

As a newspaper contributor, Sarah got to know the young editor of another paper in town, the *Madison Herald* (later called the *Madison Courier*). The editor's name was Nathaniel Bolton.

Nathaniel was born in Chillicothe, Ohio, in 1803. His father died when he was a baby, and soon afterward, his mother married printer George Smith. Nathaniel grew up working in his stepfather's printing office in Chillicothe. In 1821, when Nathaniel was eighteen, the family moved to the newly founded city of Indianapolis, which had just been named the state capital. At this early stage, much of the planned town was still forested, with underbrush too thick to walk through. George Smith had bought two of the first lots in Indianapolis, on a street that was yet to be paved and was still dotted with tree stumps. Here, in their freshly built one-room log cabin home, Nathaniel and his stepfather opened a printing shop and launched the city's first newspaper, the *Indianapolis Gazette*. After a few years, Smith took a position as a judge in Indianapolis and left the publishing of the *Gazette* to his stepson.

In 1829 Nathaniel left the *Gazette* and moved to Madison to start a new newspaper, the *Madison Herald*. A short time later, he met and befriended young Sarah Bolton. The friendship grew, and when Sarah was sixteen, Nathaniel asked her to marry him, and she agreed. Nathaniel sold his interest in the *Herald* in 1830, and right after their wedding in October 1831, the couple moved to a dairy farm just outside Indianapolis. The property belonged to Nathaniel's stepfather, George Smith, but he was unable to take care of the farm.

Nathaniel and Sarah rode the eighty miles from Madison to their new home on horseback. The couple's farmhouse was a hodgepodge of renovations. The oldest part of the house was made of plain, rough logs, while a newer section was built with square-cut logs, and the newest addition was made of modern sawed lumber.

Two years later, after getting the farm going, Nathaniel returned to the newspaper business, becoming the editor of the *Indiana Democrat* in Indianapolis. The Boltons bought a second home in town so Nathaniel would be closer to his job. Sarah and Nathaniel's first child, Sarah Ada (called Sallie), was born in the city in 1836. Nathaniel's stepfather died the same year.

Because Nathaniel had been a successful businessman from a young age, he had acquired considerable wealth and property by the time he moved back to Indianapolis, and he was very generous with his money. When friends with inadequate credit needed to borrow money at the bank, Nathaniel signed their loan papers for them. But when these friends could not pay back the money, Nathaniel, having signed the papers, was stuck with paying off the loan. Due to these debts, he was in danger of losing the farm, so in 1836 he quit his job at the *Democrat* and returned to farming, hoping to save the property. The Boltons sold dairy products, but the income from this small enterprise was inadequate.

Because the farm was located along the main road out of Indianapolis, the National Road (which later became U.S. Highway 40), Nathaniel and Sarah had many visitors, both friends and professional acquaintances. Among these visitors were state legislators and other prominent Hoosiers. But the Boltons could not afford to lodge, feed, and entertain so many people for free. Soon they came up with an idea: they could open on their property an inn—or tavern, as such lodging places were called then—and charge visitors for their room and meals. Nathaniel built a large room of peeled logs and put a sign up over the door, "Tavern by Nathaniel Bolton."

The tavern immediately became a popular gathering spot for the young people of Indianapolis. In the evenings, Nathaniel played music for his guests, and Sarah, a marvelous hostess and a beloved personality, served great food. The Boltons also held special events, such as dances and boat rides. When the Indiana General Assembly was in session, the tavern was constantly busy. Sarah and Nathaniel's son, James Pendleton Bolton, was born during this period, in 1838.

It was customary to celebrate the birth of a child by planting a tree. But Nathaniel was so overjoyed at the birth of his son that he planted a row of beech trees along each side of the long driveway from the National Road (now Washington Street) to their home. Many of these trees still stand today.

Over the Bolton Tavern's nine years of operation, many famous and important people visited. Among them were Stephen A. Douglas, U.S senator from Illinois, who later ran for president against Abraham Lincoln; James Whitcomb, who would become the governor of Indiana in 1843 and later a U.S. senator; and Jesse D. Bright, Sarah's former classmate from Madison, who would serve as Whitcomb's lieutenant governor and later as a U.S. senator. Other renowned guests included the influential newspaper editor Horace Greeley, who in 1854 would help found the Republican Party, and Indiana legislator Robert Dale Owen, son of Robert Owen, founder of the utopian New Harmony colony in southwestern Indiana. As a U.S. Congressman in the 1840s, the younger Owen would spearhead the establishment of the Smithsonian Institution in Washington, D.C.

During these years, Sarah wrote very few new poems, being so busy with other things. She had two young children to care for, ten cows to milk, butter and cheese to make, and a household to run, in addition to all the cooking, cleaning, and organizing events for the inn. She did, however, compose a poem occasionally to commemorate an important event, such as a visit by an eminent person, a wedding, or a funeral. Once in a while, she wrote a poem in response to a political development. For example, in support of Texas's struggle for independence from Mexico, she penned a poem called "Texas."

After nine years of hard work running the dairy farm and tavern, the Boltons were still in debt, so Sarah and Nathaniel concluded that they would have to sell their beloved farm. In 1845 they sold their one hundred scenic acres to the state of Indiana, which built a hospital on the property. Central State Hospital cared for people with mental illness for 146 years before finally closing in 1994.

Once the farm was sold, Sarah and Nathaniel moved back to Indianapolis. Nathaniel found a job as a secretary and custodian for the Indiana General Assembly. After the move, Sarah had more free time, and she began to write poetry regularly again. She was in the news in 1848, when the Freemasons announced that she would read a poem she had written especially for the dedication of the cornerstone of their new Masonic temple downtown.

Although no longer running an inn, the Boltons still had many politicians visiting their small home for dinner and conversation. Having so many statesmen around, Sarah became increasingly interested in the politics of the day. By 1850, the slavery issue was foremost on most Americans' minds, and there was a potential civil war in the making. Sarah was sure that neither the North nor the South could do well without the other. She wrote a poem about these worries called "The Union." Here are a few lines:

> Dissolve the Union! In the day, the hour
> Ye rend the blood-cemented tie in twain,
> The fearful cloud of civil war will lower
> O'er every old blue hill and sunny plain,
> From torrid Mexico to frigid Maine. . . .

Dissolve the Union! No! Ye can not part
With idle words the blessed ties that bind
In one the interests of that mighty heart
That treasures up the hopes of all mankind. . . .
To waver now is little less than crime;
To battle for the right is glorious, is sublime.

These lines show why Sarah's poems were popular. She wrote about things that mattered to the public, with picturesque words, strong rhymes, and a galloping rhythm.

While she continued composing poetry, Sarah also pursued her interest in politics. She often talked with state legislator Robert Dale Owen, a frequent visitor to the Bolton home. Owen was helping to write a new constitution for the state of Indiana. He believed that the constitution should declare that women, including married women, had the right to own their own property and to control any money they earned. Naturally, Sarah agreed. She decided to help Owen advance his goal by holding meetings with the wives of lawmakers, encouraging them to discuss the issue of women's rights with their husbands. Many of these ladies went further, writing letters to newspapers around the state in support of women's property rights. Many men were opposed to the idea, however, and in the end, the new Indiana constitution was finalized in 1851 without a provision for women's property rights.

The issue was not dead, however. Two years after the constitution was adopted, thanks to Sarah and the other women's activism, as well as to Robert Dale Owen himself, a law was passed ensuring Hoosier women's right to own property.

In January 1851, the Indiana General Assembly elected Nathaniel Bolton the State Librarian. According to State Historian Jacob Piatt Dunn, Nathaniel won because Sarah was so popular with the public. In support of that theory, Dunn notes that two senators voted for Sarah herself, even though her name was not on the ballot.

Sarah helped her husband in his new job, which included not only taking care of the books and records that belonged to the state, but also maintaining the building. When Govenor Joseph Wright wanted new carpets installed in the capitol in time for an upcoming meeting of governors from several states, the task fell to Nathaniel. Accompanying her husband, Sarah hurried to Cincinnati to buy the 300 yards of carpet that were needed. When they got back, they had only a few days to get it fitted, cut, sewn, and placed on the floors. Unable to find workers who knew how to sew carpeting, Sarah took on the job by herself.

For ten days and nights, she sat on the floor, cutting and stitching together strips of carpet by hand. While she worked, ideas came to her as verses of a poem. As she thought up each verse, she would stop and write it down. At the end of the ten days, the long strips of carpet were all joined, and so were the verses of her poem, which she called "Paddle Your Own Canoe."

Published in national newspapers, "Paddle Your Own Canoe" became Sarah's most famous poem. Like some of her other poems, it was later set to music, and the sheet music became a bestselling song for people to play on their pianos. Eventually the poem was translated into eight languages, and soon the name Sarah Bolton was known around the world.

In 1853, as Nathaniel's term as State Librarian was coming to a close, Sarah's old schoolmate Jesse Bright, now a U.S. senator, appointed Nathaniel to a position as a clerk for the U.S. Senate. Nathaniel moved to Washington, D.C., while Sarah and the children stayed in Indianapolis, though they visited him frequently. By this time, Sarah's poetry was appearing regularly in national newspapers.

The Boltons did not stay long in Washington, however. Less than two years later, in 1855, President Franklin Pierce appointed Nathaniel U.S. Consul to Geneva, Switzerland. Sarah and her daughter, Sallie, went with him to Europe. Sarah enjoyed the family's time overseas. While there, she and Nathaniel visited the Paris World Fair and the French Court, where they were introduced to Napoleon III and the Empress Eugenie. Sarah also took Sallie, now age twenty, to art museums and historic sites in Switzerland, Germany, Italy, and England. Sarah particularly liked Rome, which she called "the museum of the world, the record of ages, the glory of genius." Her travels inspired more poems, and the travel notes that she sent to the Indianapolis newspapers were popular reading back home.

In 1857 Sarah and Sallie returned to Indianapolis. In July Sarah received a letter from Nathaniel, still in Switzerland, saying he was very ill, and Sarah rushed back to Geneva. After a few months, Nathaniel was still ailing, so he and Sarah returned to Indiana. Only a few months later, in November of 1858, Nathaniel died. Sarah was crushed, but she persevered. She would live for thirty-five more years.

In April 1861 the Civil War broke out, and Sarah wrote poems about the fears and pain of that terrible conflict. In July of that year Sallie, who had married a man named Francis Smith, had a son, Bolton Smith. Then, in December 1861, Sarah's son James got married. Sadly, Sarah's happiness at her children's joy was short-lived. Only two years later, in November 1863, her adored daughter died after a sudden illness. Sarah expressed her grief in a poem about meeting Sallie in heaven, one verse of which said:

> And there, where the ransomed dwell,
> And the weary find repose,
> I shall meet the darling I loved so well,
> With a love that tongue can never tell—
> That only a mother knows.

Upon Sallie's death, Sarah took over the care of her little grandson, Bolton. In September 1863, Sarah married Judge Addison Reese of Missouri. She lived with Judge Reese in northeastern Missouri for only two years before ending the marriage and returning to Indiana.

Over the next few years, Sarah moved several times to different homes in the Indianapolis area, finally settling in 1871 on a beautiful fifty-five-acre estate outside the city, calling it Beech Bank. Later that year, she took Bolton, now about ten years old, to Europe to show him the sights and to find him a good school. She enrolled him in a school in Dresden, Germany, and took an apartment for herself nearby. Two years later, she returned to Beech Bank, leaving Bolton at school in Dresden. A year later she went to Europe again to check on her grandson, now in a school in Geneva.

After a year of touring the Continent, Sarah returned to Beech Bank for good. Besides Bolton, she had a number of other grandchildren by now, the children of her son James, and she enjoyed spending time with them in her later years. Finally, on August 5, 1893, Sarah T. Barrett Bolton, age seventy-eight, died peacefully at home. She was buried in Crown Hill Cemetery in Indianapolis.

In 1930 Sarah's home of Beech Bank was purchased by the city of Beech Grove, who made the property into a public park dedicated to her. Sarah's life is also commemmorated with a 1941 bronze relief plaque in the Indiana Statehouse.

Sarah Bolton saw a lot of changes over her lifetime, both in her own beloved Indiana and in the world. These lines from her poem "Our Pioneers" express her feelings about the changes she witnessed in Indianapolis from the time she moved there as a young bride to the predawn of the twentieth century:

These olden times have passed away
and in the clearing by the wood,
fair architecture stands today,
proud mansions where the cabin stood,
and cities lift their domes and spires
where hunters struck their lone camp-fires.

Zerelda Wallace (1817–1901) in her later years
—Courtesy General Lew Wallace Study and Museum

ZERELDA WALLACE

Suffragist and Temperance Advocate

From her father, Zerelda Gray Sanders Wallace gained the medical knowledge of a doctor; from her husband and stepsons, the legal knowledge of a lawyer; from her family, the religious devotion of a clergyman; and through the encouragement of her friends, the public-speaking skills of a politician. All her life, Zerelda showed a special gift for helping people get along when they disagreed by showing them what they had in common. But in spite of her abilities, due to the laws of her time, she could not vote. So, in addition to fulfilling her family responsibilities, Zerelda worked to change the laws.

Zerelda Gray Sanders was born in Millersburg, Kentucky, near Lexington, in 1817. Both of her parents came from prominent families and were well educated. Her father was Dr. John H. Sanders, a physician, and her mother was Mary "Polly" Chalfant Gray Sanders. Zerelda was the eldest of five daughters. She and her sisters—Sarah Agnes (who went by her middle name), Nancy, Mary Elizabeth, and Jemima—were lucky. Their father believed that girls had as much right as boys to a good education. He sent his daughters to school whenever he could and encouraged them to read from his extensive library.

As a very young child, Zerelda was taught the alphabet by her mother, who pasted letters from a spelling book onto a wood shingle, which Zerelda then copied. From these exercises, Zerelda learned to read and write. When she was older, Zerelda attended a local school for a few years, where she learned basic history, geography, and arithmetic. Agnes and Nancy, the two eldest of her younger sisters, no doubt attended the same school when they were old enough. When Zerelda was ten, her parents paid for her to attend a small nearby school run by a Massachusetts woman, Miss Childs, who taught English grammar. The following year, they sent her to a good boarding school in Versailles, Kentucky, for two years. There she studied history, philosophy, mythology, astronomy, rhetoric, and English composition.

Throughout her school years, Zerelda was further educated at home. Her mother taught her and her three younger sisters (the youngest, Jemima, was not born until Zerelda was twenty years old) the domestic skills they would need as adult women, such as cooking, sewing, knitting, and needlework, as well as grooming and good Southern manners. These lessons were not very interesting to Zerelda, but she would make good use of them later.

In 1830, when Zerelda was thirteen, John Sanders decided to move his family to the nine-year-old city of Indianapolis and set up his medical practice there. Zerelda's sisters Agnes and Nancy were sent to a boarding school in Cincinnati (sister Mary Elizabeth was only five), while Zerelda attended a private school in Indianapolis operated by a local Baptist minister. By this time, however, Zerelda's main teacher was her father, who began to take her with him to his medical office and on visits to his patients, which he made on horseback. The teenager became a competent nurse to her physician father, and she showed an avid interest in medicine and other advanced subjects, especially history, politics, and religion. She also enjoyed novels and other literature. Zerelda studied on her own, using Dr. Sanders's books and books borrowed from other adults, and she often discussed the material with her father and his well-educated friends.

During this period, Zerelda's family helped form a new church in Indianapolis, the First Church of Christ (later renamed Central Christian Church), a congregation of the Church of Christ denomination, later known as Disciples of Christ. Zerelda became a founding member of the church at age fifteen, and she remained with the denomination for the rest of her life. Among other things, the church taught that a person must do all that he or she can to make the world a better place for everybody.

Among the Sanders family's friends and acquaintances in Indianapolis was the lieutenant governor of Indiana, Colonel David Wallace. David's wife had died of tuberculosis in 1833, and he had three young sons. Not long after he met the curly-haired, dark-eyed Zerelda, the widower asked her to be his wife, and on Christmas Day 1936, nineteen-year-old Zerelda Sanders married thirty-seven-year-old David Wallace, becoming stepmother to David's sons—William, age eleven, Lewis (Lew), age nine, and Edward, age five.

William and Edward were happy to have a young new mother, but Lew missed his own mother and did not want anyone to take her place. One day, soon after Zerelda moved in, Lew ran away to the woods and did not return for two days. He came back crying, coughing, and feverish—he was very sick with croup. Without scolding him, Zerelda put him to bed. As Lew later remembered, "She . . . nursed me with infinite skill and tenderness. I had sense enough to know she was the savior of my life, and called her mother. And in speech and fact, mother she has been to me ever since."

Lew Wallace was a rowdy youngster, but he went on to do great things in his life. He became a lawyer, a Union general in the Civil War, the governor of the New Mexico Territory, and a famous author. His most successful book was *Ben-Hur: A Tale of the Christ*, published in 1880. Lew stated that the character of the warm, loving mother was based on Zerelda. The story was made into a silent film twice (in 1907 and 1925) and a full-color Hollywood epic in 1959. As of this writing, a new remake of *Ben-Hur* is due for release in 2016.

The Wallaces' first year of marriage, 1837, was an eventful one. In May, Zerelda's baby sister, Jemima, arrived in the world, and Zerelda's own child, Mary, was born only a few months later, making Mary nearly the same age as her aunt. In October, David was elected governor. When he took office in December, Zerelda, twenty years old, became the youngest woman ever to be First Lady of Indiana.

During David's two-year term, both the state and the nation were going through a bad time. A financial panic in 1837 had caused economic chaos thoughout the country, and Indiana, in particular, was struggling. The state could not afford to finish all the road- and canal-building projects that the previous governor, Noah Noble, had begun. Even though the state's debts had accumulated under Governor Noble, the public blamed David Wallace for the budget shortfalls and the cancellation of the public-improvement projects. In 1839 his party, the Whigs, discouraged him from running for a second term.

Instead, David ran for a seat in the United States Congress. He won the election in 1841, and Zerelda went with him to Washington, D.C., where she learned how the national government operated. David ran for re-election but was defeated, having served only one two-year term. After David's time in Congress, he and Zerelda returned to Indiana, where David went back to practicing law. Later he became a judge in Marion County.

A friend said that David and Zerelda read every book and newspaper together, and together listened to every speech and sermon. Zerelda helped David in all his work, whatever he did. Everything David wrote, he gave to Zerelda to approve or correct.

By the time Zerelda returned to Indianapolis, her two older stepsons—William and Lew—were nearly grown. Both wanted to become lawyers like their father, and Zerelda helped them study for the bar examination. Having assisted her husband in his work as governor and congressman, and having helped her sons study legal texts, Zerelda knew more than most people do about politics and the law. She would use this knowledge later, and very effectively, in her fight for women's rights.

In 1845 Zerelda gave birth to her second daughter, Ellen. Sadly, Ellen died before her first birthday. Zerelda's third child, Agnes, was born in 1849; three years later, David Jr. was born; little Jemima arrived in 1854; and Sanders, the youngest, was born in 1857. After enduring baby Ellen's death, Zerelda saw two more of her children pass away—like Ellen, Sanders died around age one, and Jemima died at age twelve. Zerelda's father also died during this period, in 1851. And in 1859, another tragedy befell Zerelda and her family: on September 4, David Wallace Sr. died suddenly of unknown causes.

David's investments had not done well, so Zerelda, age forty-two, was left with little money to support her children. In those days, there were very few job opportunities for women, so Zerelda did what she could to get by. She opened her home to boarders, renting out a few rooms and serving the tenants meals for a modest price. She also made some careful investments, and eventually the family was back on its feet.

In 1860, the year after David's death, Zerelda's eldest daughter, Mary, married William Leathers. Over the next decade, the couple had four children. In 1871, shortly after the birth of her last child, Mary died suddenly at age thirty-four. Zerelda took Mary's four children—James, age ten; Wallace, age seven; Zerelda, age five; and Mary, the infant—into her home and brought them up. All four lived to adulthood. Of Zerelda's own two surviving children, both were still single at the time of Mary's death; Agnes, age twenty-two, was living with her mother (she would marry John Steiner in 1877), and she very likely helped Zerelda with the children; David Jr., nineteen, worked for the railroad (he would marry Zelda Sequin in 1880).

In the 1870s, while she was still raising her grandchildren, Zerelda began to take an interest in some of the larger issues the nation was facing. She turned her attention to the rampant abuse of alcohol among men, which had become a severe problem for women and families, especially poor ones. Few women drank in those days, but many men of the era were heavy drinkers. If a husband spent all his money on liquor, there was nothing left for food or clothes or housing, and the wife could do nothing about it. A woman had no legal right to the money earned by her husband, and married women could seldom get regular jobs of their own, even with their husbands' permission (which was rarely given anyway). Divorces were difficult to get, and even if a woman was granted one, there was usually no place for her and her children to go. The only solution, it seemed to many women, was to ban the sale of alcohol throughout the United States. This idea, known as prohibition, was one that gained increasing support in the late nineteenth and early twentieth centuries.

In the meantime, however, many women (and men) who opposed alcohol focused on persuading individuals to refrain from drinking as a personal choice. This was called temperance. Temperance advocates generally supported laws that restricted the sale of alcohol, but they did not necessarily lobby for total nationwide prohibition, at least not at first. Instead, they attempted to change men's attitudes toward drinking, most often appealing to their religious sentiments—faith, they believed, would not only convince them to stop drinking in the first place but also keep them from relapsing into drinking again.

Zerelda embraced the idea of temperance. Deeply religious, she never drank alcohol herself. She even refused to drink communion wine in church. One day she stood up in church to explain her reasons for not drinking, and soon after, the parishioners decided to use grape juice for communion instead. Eventually the Disciples of Christ and many other Protestant congregations adopted the grape juice alternative.

When Zerelda heard that some women were forming a new organization devoted to temperance, she wanted to be a part of it. The convention to officially form the Women's Christian Temperance Union (WCTU) met in Cleveland, Ohio, in 1874, and Zerelda attended as a delegate from Indiana. In its early days, this organization tried to help underprivileged families by teaching parents about religion, hoping that Christian devotion would persuade fathers to stop drinking. At the convention, WCTU chapters in several states were organized. Zerelda took charge of the Indiana chapter and was elected its president.

At first Zerelda, a naturally shy person, had a hard time speaking in front of people. Once when she was supposed to give a speech, she got so nervous that she choked and just sat back down. But she kept trying, getting better and better at giving speeches. Soon people were saying that Zerelda was the best speaker in the state. Her talks were both reasonable and spirited.

As president of the Indiana chapter of the WCTU, Zerelda focused on promoting temperence laws in her own state. A law that limited liquor sales in saloons had been passed in Indiana in 1873. Known as the Baxter Law, it said, among other things, that alcohol could not be sold on Sundays, holidays, or election days, and all saloons must close at 9 p.m. It also said that a person wishing to open a drinking establishment in a particular town had to have his application signed by a majority of the voters of that town. No sooner had the law passed than strong objections to it emerged, especially from businesses that produced and sold alcohol, and the pressure to repeal it began.

Zerelda helped compose a petition urging state lawmakers to uphold the Baxter law and, further, asking them to add an amendment requiring saloon applicants to get the signatures of not only the town's voters but also its adult women residents. She and other volunteers combed the state gathering signatures to present to the Indiana General Assemby (state legislature). In the petition, the women were careful to say that they were not trying to gain suffrage (the right to vote; also called enfranchisement), they only wanted to have a say in the granting of local liquor licenses. This statement was added because the WCTU did not want the legislators' strong feelings against women voting to doom their effort. Some women, including May Wright Sewall, later a famous suffrage activist, refused to sign the petition because of this wording. Only a few years later, Zerelda would join May Sewall in the fight for women's enfranchisement and work closely with her to further the cause in Indiana and nationally.

Although May Wright Sewall did not sign Zerelda's petition, more than 20,000 Indiana women did sign it. In January of 1875, Zerelda, representing the "Temperence Women of Indiana," presented the petition to the Indiana General Assembly, pointing out that since women were affected by alcohol as much as (if not more than) men were, their voices deserved to be heard. She was taken aback when the legislators were openly rude to her. One lawmaker told her that the signatures of 20,000 women meant no more to the legislature than the tracks of 20,000 mice. Another said that his job was to represent the voters, and the voters did not want limits on liquor sales. Zerelda knew that this was only true because the voters were men. At that moment, it became clear to her that because women could not vote, their opinions did not count. She said to the senator, "You are against our cause, but I am grateful to you because you have made me a woman-suffragist." From that day on, Zerelda Wallace dedicated herself to fighting for voting rights.

At the WCTU convention the following year, held in Cincinnati, Zerelda was chosen chairman of the Committee on Resolutions. She proposed a resolution declaring that both men and women, regardless of race, should be able to vote on laws regulating liquor sales:

> Resolved, that since women are the greatest sufferers from the liquor traffic, and realizing that it is to be ultimately suppressed by means of the ballot, we, the Christian women of this land, in convention assembled, do pray Almighty God, and all good and true men, that the question of the prohibition of the liquor traffic shall be submitted to all adult citizens, irrespective of race, color or sex.

In those days, the idea of tying the temperance crusade to the women's suffrage movement was a new one. To many WCTU members, the concept of women voting was too radical. Nevertheless, the resolution was passed "without debate, by an almost unanimous vote" among the assembled women, according to an observer. It was only approved, as one writer put it, because "the personal charm of . . . [Mrs.] Wallace and her disarming manner of presenting the measure had made it sound desirable."

In spite of these mixed opinions, the WCTU would add women's voting rights, along with other social reforms, to its agenda in 1879, under the leadership of newly elected president Frances Willard. At that point, many of the members who disapproved of women's suffrage left the WCTU to join temperance groups that did not advocate for it. Yet the WCTU continued to grow in strength and influence, and eventually, to many women, the two issues became nearly inseparable.

In the meantime, in the spring of 1878, twenty-six women and men met at Zerelda Wallace's home and organized the Indianapolis Equal Suffrage Society (ESS), electing Zerelda as their first president. The stated purpose of the group, which included May Wright Sewall, was to work for "equal rights at the ballot-box for all citizens on the same conditions." The society held public meetings, passed out leaflets, talked to legislators, wrote letters, and arranged for national suffrage leaders to give talks in Indianapolis.

Zerelda and the ESS did not limit their lobbying efforts to state lawmakers. In 1880 Zerelda spoke before a U.S. Senate Judiciary Committee meeting on female enfranchisement. "It is not the woman question that brings us before you today," she said, "it is the human question. . . . You have attempted to do an impossible thing, to represent the whole by one-half, and because we are the other half we ask you to recognize our rights as citizens of this republic."

By 1881, most Hoosiers had come to believe that women should have the right to vote, and the suffragists' prospects looked very promising. That year, the Indiana legislature approved a measure to amend the state constitution to grant women the vote. To be ratified, however, the amendment needed to pass a second time at the next General Assembly, and then finally be approved by Indiana voters.

In advance of the legislature's second vote in 1883, Zerelda and her colleagues went to work arranging meetings, writing letters and articles, mailing postcards, and giving speeches. But Indiana's alcohol industry feared that if women got the vote, they would shut down all the saloons, so liquor dealers, bar owners, and other temperance opponents did everything they could to stop the amendment.

Unfortunately, in the end, the liquor interests prevailed. When the Indiana legislature met in 1883, the woman-suffrage amendment was never brought up for a second vote.

Zerelda and the others did not give up, though. Another amendment proposal was submitted to Indiana legislators in 1885, and many others would be presented in the 1890s and into the twentieth century. Few could have foreseen that it would take until 1920 for women to win this basic civil right.

Assisting with Zerelda's efforts in Indiana was the American Woman Suffrage Association (AWSA), one of two major nationwide women's-rights organizations. The other was the National Woman Suffrage Association (NWSA). The two groups, both formed in 1869, represented different factions with conflicting ideas about what women's rights should be and what was the best way to obtain them. The AWSA focused on local and state suffrage efforts, while the NWSA concetrated on securing women's voting rights on a national level.

Zerelda and others felt that for the movement to succeed, the two associations needed to work together. In an 1883 speech at the NWSA, Zerelda described how both groups' efforts were necessary for success. "A national amendment is the quickest, surest, least laborious way to get the vote," she asserted. "But work in the states is necessary for education." Finally, in 1890, the NWSA and the AWSA joined to form the National American Woman Suffrage Association, with Susan B. Anthony as its first president.

Throughout the 1880s and into the 1890s, Zerelda traveled all around the country making speeches. One talk, in Arkansas in 1889, was particularly effective. Zerelda was scheduled to speak first, on the pro side of the suffrage discussion; she was to be followed by an outspoken opponent of women voting, the Reverend Joseph Jones. According to one report, "At the close of Mrs. Wallace's eloquent address, Mr. Jones arose and announced that he was converted to his good sister's views, and would henceforth encourage rather than oppose the movement."

In 1892, Zerelda, then age seventy-five, fainted while giving a talk. After that episode, she retired from public speaking. Six years later, with her health declining, Zerelda moved in with her daughter Agnes, who was now married. Though she was physically weak, Zerelda remained mentally alert until the end of her life. Finally, on March 19, 1901, Zerelda Gray Sanders Wallace, age eighty-three, died from a lingering bronchial infection. She was buried beside her husband in Crown Hill Cemetery in Indianapolis.

Zerelda did not live to see the U.S. constitutional amendment giving women the right to vote pass in 1920, nor did she see the national amendment prohibiting alcohol ratified the same year. While Prohibition proved to be a disaster and was repealed thirteen years later, women's suffrage, a long-overdue advancement in many people's minds, turned out to be the first major step toward American women gaining full equality.

In a time when it was thought that a woman could not raise a family and also have a public life, Zerelda Wallace did both. In a time when women had no influence in political affairs, Zerelda's wisdom convinced many political leaders that her causes were just. In a time when women themselves were uncertain about their own future, Zerelda Wallace helped them understand that by working together, they had the power to change laws for the betterment of their own lives and the lives of their daughters and granddaughters.

Portrait of Lillian T. Fox (1854–1917), date unknown
—Courtesy Indiana Historical Society

LILLIAN THOMAS FOX

Journalist and Health Care Activist

In August of 1900, Lillian Thomas Fox, newly hired reporter for the *Indianapolis News*, presented a speech on "Women in Journalism" at the meeting of the Afro-American Press Association. She began with a quote from Martin Luther, leader of the sixteenth-century Protestant Reformation: "No human device holds a more exalted place in mankind's regard than does the pen." She continued, "The part that woman has taken in connection with the most worthy events [in] the world's history prompts me to say that the pen has been most efficiently wielded by women."

While it was unusual for a woman to be a journalist in those days, Lillian pointed out that she was not the first female to write about the world around her. Nor was she the first African American to speak about the social problems suffered by black citizens in the United States. She was, however, a powerful voice in her time, encouraging her fellow "Negroes" to seek education and self-improvement; commending the achievements of prominent black citizens; and calling upon African Americans to strive toward the betterment of their own communities. In fact, Lillian did more than write and speak—she also organized, worked with, and supported women's groups that advocated for civil rights and improved health care for African Americans. A prime example was her successful effort to establish a treatment center for black tuberculosis patients in Indianapolis in the early 1900s.

———————

Lillian May Parker, later known as Lillian Thomas Fox, was born in 1854, during the era of slavery, but her parents were free blacks, living in Chicago. Her mother, Jane Janette Johnson, was a schoolteacher. Her father was the famed Reverend Byrd Parker, pastor of an African Methodist Episcopal church and an accomplished speaker for the abolition of slavery and black civil rights. When he moved to Chicago, Byrd Parker worked with Frederick Douglass to help escaped slaves moving along the Underground Railroad to find safe havens in the city and prepare them for their crossing to Canada. (Even in the North, runaway slaves were not safe; to be free, they had to cross the Canadian border.) Reverend Parker also started a school for black children in Chicago. Before moving to that city, he lived in New Albany, Indiana, and before that in Louisville, Kentucky. Throughout his adult life, no matter where he called home, the reverend spent much of his time traveling through the Midwest giving his talks.

In 1855, just after Lillian, the first of Byrd and Jane Parker's three children, was born, the Parker family moved from Chicago to Oshkosh, Wisconsin. Wisconsin was a free state, and many black freemen and former slaves lived there. Lillian (her family may have called her by her middle name of May), grew up in Oshkosh with her sister, Ida, two years younger than Lillian, and her brother, Byrd Jr., about three years younger than Ida.

In Oshkosh, Reverend Parker gave up preaching and opened a restaurant, but he continued serving the black community. For example, after a bad fire downtown, he helped raise money for the people who had lost their homes or businesses. He also continued giving speeches about black voting rights around the state.

In 1860, when Lillian was six years old, Reverend Parker contracted a lung infection and died. Even though she was young when she lost him, Lillian felt the influence of her father's values and his legacy throughout her life.

Not long after Byrd Parker's death, Lillian's widowed mother remarried. Her new husband was a local barber named Robert Thomas. In addition to changing her own surname upon her marriage, Jane changed her still-young children's last names to Thomas. Eventually, Jane and Robert had four children of their own—two boys and two girls. The oldest was Dora, then came the twins, Charles Bushrod and Nannie, and finally Frank arrived in 1869, when Lillian was about fifteen. The children all attended public schools in Oshkosh. Although schools were segregated, the education offered to black students in Oshkosh was considered superior to what existed in most other places.

Lillian's first job, at age sixteen, was working as a hairdresser in Oshkosh, using skills she learned from her stepfather. Later she moved to Louisville, Kentucky, where she worked as a secretary for a transportation company. Sometime in the early 1880s, Lillian's company transferred her to its Indianapolis office. The capital city offered good opportunities for a young single woman intent on improving herself. Among other things, Lillian studied dramatic reading and public speaking at the Indiana-Boston Institute for Young Ladies in Indianapolis.

Lillian had been in Indianapolis only a short time when her stepfather, Robert Thomas, died in 1884. After Robert's death, Lillian's mother, Jane, decided to move in with her daughter in Indianapolis, as her children were all grown by then or nearly so. Lillian bought an old house in town and fixed it up for herself and her mother. Jane lived there with Lillian until her own death some ten years later.

As Lillian became more skilled at public speaking, she was sometimes hired to give dramatic readings of great literature to various community groups. After a while, she also started giving speeches on topics that affected African Americans. The local black newspapers, of which there were several, called Lillian "a versatile and graceful speaker" and lauded her as "a new star in the literary heavens." For a time, she supplemented her meager earnings as a speaker by working as a seamstress.

As the years passed and Lillian honed her communication skills, she became more and more in demand as a speaker. She also joined several black women's clubs. Women's clubs were very popular in the late nineteenth and early twentieth centuries. The various clubs, almost always segregated by race, focused on different areas. Some were literary or educational, while others were politically active; still others were merely social. Whatever the club's purpose, most clubwomen did some kind of charitable work in their community.

In 1891 Lillian was contacted by George Knox, owner of the *Indianapolis Freeman,* one of the city's black newspapers. He was impressed by her speeches, he said, and wanted to hire her as a reporter. Lillian gladly took the job.

The *Freeman,* founded in 1888, was a well-respected weekly newspaper, written and published by African Americans for the black community not only in Indianapolis but all over the country too. Among Lillian's varied duties at the paper were reading the letters that came in to the paper and deciding which ones to publish, reporting on local events, and writing several regular columns, including "Race Gleanings," "Church," "Stage," and "Friendly Reminders." At the time, she was the only woman on the *Freeman* staff.

Because the *Freeman* was published only once a week, Lillian had time to continue giving talks. She spoke to churches and political groups in Indianapolis and many other cities. One day, on a speaking trip to Pensacola, Florida, Lillian met a local tailor named James Fox. James had immigrated to Florida from Jamaica and had built a successful business in Pensacola. In 1893, when Lillian was thirty-nine years old, she married James Fox in a simple wedding at her home. The only witnesses were her mother, one of her brothers, and the minister. James moved his tailoring business to Indianapolis, setting up shop in a prominent place on Indiana Avenue, in the center of the black community. Lillian quit her job at the *Indianapolis Freeman,* though she continued to work with her women's clubs.

Lillian was still a newlywed when her happiness was cut short. In 1894 both her mother and her half-brother Charles Bushrod, suffering from tuberculosis, died within days of each other. Tuberculosis (TB) was a common lung disease among poor people, including African Americans, who lived in crowded housing with poor sanitation. There was no treatment for TB in the 1890s other than fresh air, sunlight, nutritious food, and lots of rest. Some people recovered from TB, especially if they had proper care, but many died.

A building on the grounds of the Indianapolis City Hospital was devoted to tuberculosis patients, but it was not open to black people. There were no medical facilities for Lillian's mother and brother. She could only take care of them herself at home, watching them get sicker and sicker, feverish and coughing up blood, until they died. She would not forget the terrible experience and the tragic consequences of segregated health care.

A year after Lillian's mother and brother died, it became clear that her marriage to James Fox was not working out. Adding to whatever personal troubles came between them, James was unable to earn a living as a tailor in Indianapolis. Before the couple's second anniversary, James left Lillian and returned to Florida.

Suddenly alone and unemployed, Lillian went back to her work as a speaker. Among the groups she spoke to were the Afro-American Council, the Atlanta Congress of Colored Women, the National Association of Colored Women's Clubs, the Bethel African Methodist Episcopal Literary Society, and various other clubs and churches. It's worth noting that the terms "colored" and "Negro" for black people were not derogatory or offensive in the early twentieth century; in fact, they were polite and even respectful terms, used by African Americans themselves until the 1970s. While they are old-fashioned expressions, it is only their association with the days of segregation that makes them seem demeaning to modern ears.

To give her talks, Lillian did more and more traveling. During one 1895 train trip to Atlanta, she had a bad but all-too-common experience for African Americans in those days. It was similar to what would happen to Rosa Parks sixty years later. Traveling from Indianapolis to a convention in Atlanta, Lillian had a first-class ticket on the Southern Railroad. When the train stopped at Chattanooga,

Tennessee, near the Georgia state line, a new conductor took over. It was late at night.

The new conductor, a white man, told Lillian she had to leave the first-class car and move to the Negro section in the smoking car. Lillian replied, "I have paid for this seat, and I will remain in this seat."

Angered, the conductor shot back, "Then I will carry you to the baggage car. Or throw you off the train."

"If you do that," Lillian said calmly, "I promise you, it will be the most expensive job you have ever done for your employers." In other words, if he continued harassing her, she would sue the railroad.

Lillian Thomas Fox was a well-known and respected speaker, but that didn't matter to the white train conductor. When Lillian wouldn't budge, the conductor stopped the train and threw her suitcase and lunchbox out onto the ground. Having no choice, she got up to retrieve her things, and when she stepped off, the conductor signaled for the train to pull away, leaving her in the middle of nowhere at midnight.

Seeing this, some of the white passengers cried out for the conductor to stop the train, and he did. He let Lillian back on, but he forced her to sit in the back car the rest of the way to Atlanta. When she got home, Lillian followed up on her threat to sue the Southern Railroad. It is unknown, however, whether or not she won the lawsuit.

In 1900 the *Indianapolis News,* a mainstream, white-owned daily paper, contacted Lillian about a job. They wanted her to write a column called "News of the Colored Folk." She accepted the offer, becoming the first African American to write for a white newspaper in Indiana.

In her column, Lillian listed upcoming meetings and events of black organizations and related news from the black community. Among the things she reported on were lobbying efforts for civil-rights laws; the opening of a rescue home for black girls in trouble; and the progress of local black-owned businesses. She also wrote features about successful local black doctors, dentists, accountants, and lawyers, as well as nationally prominent African Americans. Lillian wanted readers, both black and white, to know what African Americans were doing to help themselves and their communities. Her column was very popular. Over time, the *News* gave Lillian more and more space until she was writing a whole page every day by herself.

Although Lillian was very busy during that period of her life, she wanted to do more. In 1903, at age forty-nine, she formed a club for educated and affluent black women called the Colored Women's Improvement Club (later shortened to the Women's Improvement Club, or WIC). The group included organization leaders, public speakers, and members of such civil-rights groups as the Afro-American Council and the Anti-Lynching League. Some of the women were professionals, working as teachers, nurses, or social workers; others were the wives of successful businessmen or professionals. All had exceptional skills, energy, and community spirit. The club limited its membership to twenty women, so it was an honor to be invited to join the WIC.

A particularly notable member of the WIC was Dr. Beulah Wright Porter. Beulah started out as a schoolteacher before attending medical school. In 1897 she became the first black female physician in Indianapolis. After only a few years, however, she gave up her medical practice because she could not make a living as a doctor. This may seem strange, but since she treated mostly African Americans, many of her patients may have been too poor to pay much for her services. It's also possible that people were reluctant to see a woman physician. In any case, Beulah went back to teaching, later becoming a public-school principal.

In 1905 Lillian and Beulah teamed up to open an outdoor summer camp for black Hoosiers with TB, the disease that had claimed Lillian's mother and brother. The WIC collected donations of money, materials, and labor from black and white churches and community groups and black- and white-owned businesses. William Haueisen, a local white businessman, offered the WIC a spot on his

The tuberculosis camp at Oak Hill, circa 1905 —Courtesy Indiana Historical Society

country estate, Oak Hill, for the camp. It opened with three tents for six patients, plus volunteers to prepare meals, do laundry, and attend to the patients' needs. It was the first outdoor TB convalescence camp, white or black, in the nation. It was also the only place in Indianapolis where black patients could get treatment for TB until 1909, when Ward's Sanitarium, the first African American hospital in Indianapolis, opened. Both Beulah and Lillian were also actively involved in establishing the Sisters of Charity Hospital, which opened in 1911 to treat black patients.

The Oak Hill camp operated until 1916. After Lillian's retirement from the WIC in 1914, the group continued to struggle for funding for the camp, but without Lillian's leadership, the women finally had to give up on it and move on to other projects.

Another important project the WIC took on was establishing a nurses' training program for black students. Any African American in Indianapolis who wanted to be a nurse had to go to Chicago or Kalamazoo, Michigan, for training because the local nursing schools did not admit people of color. The WIC's program was taught by the head nurse from City Hospital, Indianapolis's only major medical facility that admitted black patients along with white ones (though its TB clinic was closed to African Americans until 1917).

In addition to her work with the WIC, Lillian was the lead organizer of the Indiana Federation of Colored Women's Clubs, which combined the forces and resources of at least fourteen black women's groups to work to improve education, health care, and living conditions for African American Hoosiers. The federation's first meeting was held in 1904. Affiliated with the National Association of Colored Women's Clubs, the IFCWC also addressed larger political issues, such as black voter suppression, racial discrimination, and lynching. The IFCWC clubhouse is now on the National Register of Historic Places.

In subsequent years, while still reporting for the *Indianapolis News*, Lillian continued to help organize clubs and associations, founding the Woman's Civic Club (WCC) of Indianapolis in 1907, which led to the founding of the Indianapolis chapter of the National Association for the Advancement of Colored People (NAACP) in 1912. The WCC organized cultural events, such as inviting black artists to speak and display their work. In 1913, under the sponsorship of the WIC and the WCC, Lillian wrote, directed, and produced a satiric play about race relations called *The Temple of Progress* as a fundraiser. She was also an organizing member of the Indianapolis Anti-Lynching League.

After all this activity, Lillian's health began to weaken and she was losing her vision. Finally in 1914, at the age of sixty, she retired from the *News* and from her club work. Three years later, in 1917, Lillian suffered a stroke and died at the home of a friend. She was buried in Crown Hill Cemetery in Indianapolis.

The work begun by Lillian Thomas Fox was continued by the people she had inspired. The WIC persisted in its fight against tuberculosis in Indianapolis's black community. In 1916 the club participated in the opening of a "fresh air" school for black children to prevent TB. The following year, thanks largely to the lobbying of the WIC, Indianapolis City Hospital finally established a TB ward for Negro patients. A free TB clinic for African Americans was launched in 1919 at Flanner House, a black community service center established 1898, and in 1920 the Board of Health opened another free TB clinic in the city for black patients. Even so, tubercular African Americans in Indianapolis needed more. For instance, the city had no facilities for the long-term care of black patients with advanced cases of TB. In 1922 the WIC took over an empty hospital and converted it into just such a facility.

During the 1920s, the WIC gradually changed its focus to health education, inviting speakers to talk about tuberculosis and other health issues in Indianapolis's black community. The club also reached out to white women's groups to work on issues of interest to all women, including women's rights, social services for poor children, and medical care for wounded soldiers.

In many ways, Lillian Thomas Fox was astounding. She overcame her era's prejudice against both women and African Americans to become a respected speaker, journalist, and community leader. She used her speaking and organizing skills to inspire the black citizens of Indiana and elsewhere to keep working toward improving the conditions of their communities. In her newspaper work, she not only reported news about Indiana's black communities for African American readers, she also enlightened white Hoosiers about the largely unsung civic accomplishments and rich culture of Indianapolis's black society. As one historian put it, "In her own way, [Lillian] built a bridge between the white and black communities of Indianapolis."

In 2014, nearly a hundred years after her death, Lillian Thomas Fox was inducted into the Indiana Journalism Hall of Fame. In an article commemorating the occasion, Wilma Moore, senior archivist of African American history at the Indiana Historical Society, summed up Lillian's legacy. "Man or woman, black or white," Moore said, "Lillian Thomas Fox's feats were extraordinary, remarkable, and exceptional. She was a true leader with grit and one of those rare souls who could write about it, talk about it, and do it."

Gene Stratton-Porter (1863–1924) in her garden in California, 1924
—Courtesy Indiana State Museum

GENE STRATTON-PORTER

Naturalist, Author, and Photographer

When Geneva Stratton was a child, her father gave her a wonderful gift. It was not the kind of gift that comes in a box with a bow on it—it was much bigger, and it captured the young girl's imagination. All the birds on the family farm, Geneva's father declared in his big voice, now belonged to her, and no one would be allowed to hurt them.

Geneva was thrilled, but she also understood that this gift came with a responsibility, which she took very seriously. She already spent most of her days wandering around the farm searching for birds and their nests, but with her father's declaration, she felt that she now needed to do more than just watch and listen to her feathered pals—she must also nurture and protect them. Every day, Geneva walked through the fields and woods to check on her birds, making sure they were safe and healthy, shooing cats and squirrels away from their nests, and even feeding the babies. Later, in her writings as Gene Stratton-Porter, she worked to teach other people to revere and safeguard birds as well as other wild animals, plants, and indeed all of nature.

Geneva Grace Stratton was born on August 17, 1863, on the Stratton family farm in Lagro, Indiana. Her family called her Geneve. Later, she further shortened her name to Gene. Geneve was the twelfth and last child born to Mark Stratton, a farmer and later a Methodist minister, and Mary Shallenberger Stratton. The couple had come to Indiana from Ohio twenty-five years earlier. By the time Geneve came along, the Stratton property, dubbed Hopewell Farm, was prospering, and Mary Stratton, a passionate gardener, had planted myriad flowers and trees all over the property. Growing up, Gene would learn much about plants from her energetic, green-thumbed mother.

Geneve had been a late arrival in the Stratton family—her father was fifty and her mother was forty-seven when she was born, and some of her older siblings were already married with children of their own. Still living at home at the time were brothers Irvin, age fifteen; Leander ("Laddie"), ten; and Lemon, seven; and sisters Florence (Flora), age twelve, and Ada, five. Her grown siblings were Catherine, Anastasia, Mary Ann, and Jerome. Two of Geneve's sisters, Louisa Jane and Samira, had died in childhood, years before she was born.

Of all her brothers and sisters, Geneve was closest to Laddie, who was always kind to her and loved the farm as much as she did. Although he was too old to play little-girl games with her, he took her with him all over the farm, teaching her the names of the plants and birds and insects. He often lifted her up so she could see a bird's nest or pick fruit from a tree.

When Geneve was five years old, her vibrant mother contracted typhoid fever, an illness from which she never completely recovered. With her mother mostly bedridden, little Geneve roamed free for much of the day, making up songs as she chased butterflies through the meadows, listening to the birds chattering as she strolled along a nearby stream, and following her brothers' plow in the crop fields, hunting for arrowheads in the turned-up dirt.

Of course, Geneve was not allowed to play all the time. In a large family like the Strattons, everyone had chores. Some of Geneve's jobs included bringing in wood chips for the kitchen stove and the fireplace, feeding the chickens and gathering eggs, and collecting certain plants for her mother, who used them to make homemade medicines.

Before she started school, Geneve was alone much of the time, but she did not seem to mind, as she entertained herself very well exploring the outdoors. Her love of birds in particular revealed itself early. As farmers, Geneve's father and brothers sometimes shot birds that were eating fruit from the orchards or killing the chickens. When she discovered this, little Geneve not only protested but intervened. One time she rescued an injured hawk her father had shot, nursed it, and kept it as a pet. During the time the Strattons were in Lagro, Geneve adopted many pet birds, including a blue jay named Hezekiah and a rooster named Bobbie.

It was from the birds that young Geneve learned about death. One of her earliest memories was the day she found a woodpecker lying motionless on the ground. She tried to wake it up by spreading its wings and tossing it in the air; she even tried putting some berries in its mouth, but the bird did not wake up. When she asked her father how to make the bird well, he told her it was dead and explained what that word meant. Upon learning that her brothers had shot the woodpecker because it was eating cherries from the orchard, Geneve promised that she would not eat any more cherries, so there would be enough for all the birds and no one would have to shoot them. Her mother told her that she did not have to stop eating cherries, because there were plenty for everyone, and she instructed her sons not to shoot any more birds. Both of Geneve's parents showed sympathy for their daughter's sensitivity toward feathered creatures. It was after she saved the hawk that Mark Stratton presented his little girl with his gift, the announcement that all the birds on Hopewell Farm were now hers.

The summer that Geneve turned six, her brother Irvin, home from college recuperating from a kick by a horse, taught his baby sister the alphabet, so by the time her parents sent her to school that fall, Geneve already knew how to read and write. Although she enjoyed reading and liked to recite poems for the family in the evening—some of which she had composed herself—in school she did not do well. This free spirit of a child hated the confinement of the classroom. Every morning, her sister Ada had to practically drag her to the small local schoolhouse in Lagro.

Although Geneve did not like school, she loved learning. Her favorite lessons were taught at home. Every evening after supper, the Stratton family gathered around the fireplace to listen to Mark Stratton read from the Bible or a history book. Sometimes he told stories from his own life or the lives of the Stratton ancestors. Geneve liked to crawl up on his lap when he read or told stories, and she often fell asleep there. Geneve's father was a very important person in her life. He taught her many skills on the farm, but most of all she learned from him how to tell a good story. Many times she heard her father say, "I would rather that one of my children wrote a book I could be proud of, than to sit on the throne of England." She never forgot that.

Unfortunately, the quiet happiness of the Stratton family was shattered in 1872, when Geneve was eight years old. In February of that year, her sister Mary Ann, age thirty-two, died from injuries she had suffered in an earlier train accident. The family was still mourning this loss when another tragedy occurred, this one far worse for Geneve. One evening in July, about a month before Geneve's ninth birthday, nineteen-year-old Laddie and a few of his friends were coming back from town when they saw some boys they knew swimming in the Wabash River. The boys challenged Laddie and his two companions to swim across the river and join them, so they took off their boots and shirts and jumped in.

But the current was too strong for them. Laddie and his best friend drowned. When Laddie's body was carried home, Geneve saw that her beloved brother was gone, and picking up his boots, she ran, hysterical, to her mother. Life was never the same after that terrible day. The whole family was stunned and grief-stricken, not least of all the youngest Stratton. Laddie was buried alongside his three sisters in the Stratton family cemetery on Hopewell Farm.

The loss of her fourth child worsened Mary Stratton's already fragile health. With his wife's increasingly severe illness, his eldest sons gone off to their own lives, and Laddie, the only Stratton boy interested in farming, dead, Mark Stratton began to wonder if the family should leave Hopewell Farm and move to the nearby town of Wabash. In 1874, after some bad crops left the family short on money, Mark Stratton leased the farm and moved, with his sickly wife and four youngest children, into the Wabash home of his daughter Anastasia and her husband, attorney Alvah Taylor. Geneve, naturally, did not want to leave the farm and all her birds. As a consolation, her father let her bring nine of her pet birds with her to their new home.

Not surprisingly, eleven-year-old Geneve was miserable in Wabash. She detested the noisy, smelly city. She didn't like living in her sister's crowded house. Most of all, she hated going to school eight months a year (the country school was open only four months a year), and she did not like the assignments the teachers gave her—she wanted to learn what interested her, not what the teachers wanted her to learn. She also felt out of place among the other kids, and she never really made any friends in Wabash.

In February 1875, only a few months after Geneve's family moved to town, Mary Stratton died. Her body was taken back to Hopewell Farm for burial next to her children, under a cedar tree she had planted herself.

It had been less than three years since Geneve lost her dearest brother, and now she had to face the death of her cherished mother. Soon after Mary's death, Mark Stratton moved out of Anastasia's home into a new place with Geneve, age twelve; Ada, seventeen; and Flora, an adult at twenty-four but still unmarried. Geneve's brother Lemon, now nineteen, stayed with Anastasia. Flora helped bring in money by giving music lessons, while Ada and Geneve, still in school, helped their sister with the housekeeping and cooking. Geneve declared that she would never get married because she didn't like housework.

Geneve's time in Wabash was not all bad. She had her birds, and she soon began collecting moths as well. By the time she was in high school, she was writing stories and poems for her own amusement. She also took painting lessons (paid for with produce from the farm) and learned to play violin, piano, and banjo from her sister Flora.

In the summers, the Stratton family often spent time at Sylvan Lake in Rome City, Indiana. An event known as a Chautauqua Assembly— an educational, religious, social, and recreational gathering popular at the time—was held there every year. Accompanied by Flora and Ada, Geneve attended her first Chautauqua in 1881, when she was almost eighteen. Finally out in nature once again, she loved it at the lake, and she was determined to return to Sylvan Lake for the Chautauqua Assembly every summer.

The next few years brought more painful changes to Geneve and her family. In 1882 Anastasia, age forty-four, was diagnosed with cancer and sent to a medical facility in Illinois. While the family was dealing with this, Florence announced she was engaged to a widower named William Compton. The couple married in October and moved to Michigan. Geneve was sorry to see her sister go. The following spring, Anastasia died, and Mark Stratton moved back into her home with Ada and Geneve to help Anastasia's husband, Alvah, and their two children. Lemon was still there. Once again, Geneve found herself in a sad and crowded household.

Throughout those turbulent years, Geneve's grades suffered. Finally, to punish her, her father made her release or give away all of her pet birds. Hurt, angry, and frustrated, Geneve, just weeks before her graduation in 1883, abruptly dropped out of high school. In the fall, another disruption occurred—Geneve's sister Ada, the closest to Geneve in age, married a man named Frank Wilson. The couple wanted to move into their own home, but the idea of Ada leaving upset Geneve. She did not want to be the only woman at her brother-in-law's house; this would place the burden on her to do the housekeeping for him and his kids as well as for her own father and brother. Feeling bad for Geneve, Ada and her groom stayed.

About a month later, Lemon, the black sheep in the Stratton family and a heavy drinker, suddenly eloped with a local girl and moved out of the house. While the family did not approve of Lemon's bride nor of his behavior, no one, including Geneve, was really sorry to see him go. The Strattons would not hear from him much after that— he spent the next few decades of his life going from place to place and job to job. His first marriage ended in divorce. His second wife, with whom he had a daughter, died, and his third wife would be his widow.

Closing out that eventful year, in December Geneve took a bad fall and cracked her skull. The doctor had to shave off all of Geneve's hair to treat the injury, and worse, she would be bedridden for months. Thanks to Ada's tender nursing, Geneve slowly recovered. She was almost but not completely well when Anastasia's husband remarried in May, obliging the Strattons to move again. They returned to the house they had previously rented in Wabash. It was around this time that Geneve shortened her name to Gene.

That summer, Gene, now almost twenty-one, was still using a cane to help her walk when she attended her next Chautauqua Assembly at Sylvan Lake. She enjoyed herself immensely at the event, unaware that she had caught the attention of a bachelor named Charles D. Porter. Charles, a pharmacist and drugstore owner from Geneva, Indiana, was intrigued by this unusual young woman with gray eyes and curly, dark brown hair. In those days, it was considered improper for a man to approach a strange woman without a formal introduction from a third party. Rather than ask someone to introduce him to Gene, Charles decided to find out her name and address and just write her a letter.

When Gene returned to Wabash, she found a surprise waiting for her—a letter from a man she did not know. A more traditional young woman might have been offended at the man's inappropriate action, but not Gene—she wrote him back right away. They began corresponding regularly, though Gene would not meet Charles face-to-face for another year.

Gene and Charles agreed to meet at the next summer's Chautauqua. The time they spent there together was clearly enjoyable for both because a few months later, in October 1885, they became engaged. Charles was a good man and a forward-thinking one. He let Gene know that he was glad to allow his wife to keep her independence. Surely, strong-willed Gene would not have agreed to marry him otherwise. The couple married in April

1886, when Gene was twenty-two and Charles was thirty-five. The newlyweds moved to Charles's hometown of Decatur, Indiana, where he'd taken over his late mother's house. Charles had moved from Geneva because Decatur was approximately halfway between his original drugstore in Geneva and the new store he'd recently opened in Fort Wayne, allowing him to travel easily to both.

A year later, Gene and Charles had a baby girl, whom they named Jeannette. Charles sold his drugstore in Fort Wayne so he would not be gone from home so much, but since he still rode the train every day from Decatur to his store in Geneva, sometimes getting home late in the evening, Gene suggested they move back to Geneva. In 1888 the Porter family settled into a small yellow house in that town.

The town of Geneva was surrounded by a huge wetland called the Limberlost Swamp. Gene soon grew to love the place. The plants and wildlife of Limberlost reignited her passion for nature. Before long, she was bringing birds, moths, and caterpillars into the house. Growing up, Jeannette learned to handle the little creatures gently.

In 1890 Gene's father, Mark Stratton, had a stroke and died. This most recent blow to Gene's well-being put her into a confused and depressed state of mind. To cope, she renewed her teenage love of music and began playing the piano and violin again. Many historians believe that she also wrote her first book at this time, though it was published anonymously and Gene never mentioned it.

By 1892 Charles Porter was doing well for himself. In addition to the success of his drugstore, oil had been discovered on several Geneva properties, including his own, and before long the quiet little town was teaming with fortune seekers. Later that year, Charles, who had always been interested in finances and banking, opened the town's first bank, Geneva Bank, which, thanks to the boom, also prospered. In 1894 Charles decided he could afford to build a larger house, which he and Gene designed themselves. It was built of cedar logs like a cabin in the woods, but with six bedrooms, a library, a music room, and a large sunroom filled with flowers, it was hardly a "cabin." Nevertheless, Charles and Gene named the place Limberlost Cabin. The house was completed in 1895 and the Porters moved in. By then, Jeannette was eight years old.

Limberlost Cabin had a number of special features, one being the sunroom, or conservatory. Shaped in a semicircle off the dining room, it had windows all around for the plants. In the daytime, Gene left the windows open for birds to fly in and out. At night she often sat in the dining room with a sketchpad and pencils, waiting for colorful moths to alight on the window panes so she could draw them.

Shortly after the Porters moved into the new house, a major fire broke out in Geneva, which had no fire department. The blaze started downtown in the middle of the night. Charles was out of town on business, so Gene was alone with Jeannette. Upon seeing the flames, Gene ran out in her slippers to help organize the townspeople to fetch water and throw it on the fire. Many buildings were lost, including Charles's drugstore, but it could have been worse. Afterward, the Geneva newspaper noted Gene's leadership, saying that she "would make an energetic chief of the fire department" whenever the town got one.

Charles quickly rebuilt his drugstore. He also invested in an expansion of the Geneva Bank. With the Porters' assets tied up in these projects, money became tight again. Rather than endure a future of financial ups and downs, Gene decided that it was time to earn her own money. But what kind of work might she do?

Clearly, Gene Stratton-Porter had expertise to share, and she was an excellent writer, so the answer was obvious—she would write about nature and sell her work to magazines. She wrote an article about the local bird life and sent it to an outdoors magazine. The publishers liked the article, but they wanted some photographs to go with it. When Gene received the photo samples the magazine sent her, however, she was horrified to see that the birds in the pictures were dead and stuffed. They did not show the bird life that she was trying to capture in her piece. She was so upset, in fact, that she refused to allow her article to appear with those photographs.

Gene's story was not published. She could not submit it elsewhere, either—there were virtually no magazines that would publish an article without illustrations, and she knew of no photos of live birds that she could use instead. The field of photography was still very young in 1895. Cameras were large and unwieldy, and the images were captured on heavy glass plates. Such equipment was difficult to move around in the outdoors. Furthermore, to get a good picture, the subject had to stay still for a long time. Therefore few photographers were willing to haul their equipment out into natural areas and try to shoot constantly moving wildlife. Gene's writing career, it seemed, was stopped cold. She did not even mention her failed attempt to Charles or Jeannette.

As fate would have it, at the Porters' first Christmas in Limberlost Cabin, Jeannette gave her mother a camera as a gift, suggesting she might like to photograph the birds and other wildlife of Limberlost Swamp. It was perfect! Gene could now take her own pictures and send them in with her articles. But first, of course, she had to learn how to use the camera. Eventually, over the course of the next year or so, Gene taught herself, mostly by trial and error, not only how to take photographs but also how to develop them, using chemicals from her husband's drugstore. The family bathroom served as her darkroom.

Gene knew that the birds would allow her to get close enough to them to get a good shot. Unlike most people, she knew how to gain their trust, having developed this skill as a child, after her father gave her the gift of the birds.

In 1900 Gene began to write articles again in earnest. If she needed photos, she took them herself. The first magazine she sent her work to was so impressed, the publishers asked her to write a regular column, called "Camera Notes," about wildlife photography. Instead of compensating her in cash, the magazine paid her with new photo equipment.

With that success, Gene began to send articles and photos to other magazines. Within a few years, her work was in demand. No one else could observe wild birds with such patience and describe them the way Gene did. No one else could take pictures of birds in their natural habitats without even disturbing them.

For his part, Charles did not like Gene going out by herself into the field, with its hazardous terrain, venomous snakes, thick underbrush, and other perils, so he occasionally went with her. One day he and Gene ventured out in search of a black vulture's nest that someone had told them about. After much slogging through the swamp, they found a large hollow log with something inside it. Sure enough, it was the vulture's nest, complete with a baby bird. After chasing the mother vulture away, Charles crawled into the log to get the baby. Most birds are very clean, but this nest smelled terrible because vultures eat dead animals, even rotting ones. The odor was so bad that Charles and Gene had to cover their noses with handkerchiefs dipped in disinfectant.

Inside the log, Charles filled his hat with leaves, gently placed the nest with the baby vulture into the hat, and brought it out so Gene could take pictures. When she finished, Charles crawled back into the smelly log and put the nest back where he had found it. The Porters visited the nest several more times, watching the baby vulture, whom they started calling "Little Chicken," grow up. Gene's article about black vultures, accompanied by her photos, was published in *Outing* magazine in December of 1901.

Earlier that year, Gene had tried her hand at fiction. In September, her first short story was published in *Metropolitan* magazine. Soon afterward, the magazine editor asked Gene to write more stories for him. Gene Stratton-Porter was now a fiction writer as well as a nature writer.

The following spring, Gene lost another family member when her brother Irvin—the one who had taught her to read—was killed in a traffic accident. She was never able to write about that painful loss, nor about the loss of her father twelve years earlier. She did, however, write. As if driven by grief, she poured herself into her work more than ever. Later that year, Gene submitted a fiction story about a family of cardinals to one of the magazines she wrote for. Impressed, the editor suggested that Gene make the story longer and have it published as a book. This she did, and her first novel, *The Song of the Cardinal,* was released by an Indiana book publisher in 1903. Gene asked that her name appear as Gene Stratton-Porter, so that everyone would know she was Mark Stratton's daughter. She remembered how her father hoped a child of his would write a book he could be proud of.

Although Gene preferred writing nonfiction, publishers and editors had told her repeatedly that novels were easier to sell than nature books. In those days, with few other modes of entertainment available, people read novels a lot. Thus Gene began to pen more fiction, though she always filled her stories and novels with descriptions of nature. Her second novel, *Freckles,* was an exciting and romantic tale about a boy in the Limberlost Swamp who found true love after bravely facing down a gang of thieves.

Published in 1904, *Freckles* was very successful, and the public began to clamor for more books by Gene Stratton-Porter. Gene did not exactly mind this, but she still yearned to write more nature books. As a compromise, she decided to write both types of books and publish them alternately, hoping the popularity of her novels would encourage more readers take a look at her nature books too.

Gene's best-known novel, *Girl of the Limberlost,* was published in 1909 and brought the author more fame than ever. Although critics rarely praised her work, the reading public adored it. By the end of her career, Gene Stratton-Porter's books had been translated into some fourteen languages and had sold an estimated five million copies worldwide.

Shortly before *Girl of the Limberlost* came out, Gene's attention turned to Jeannette, now age twenty-two, when she announced that she planned to marry a Pennsylvania oilman named G. Blaine Monroe. Neither Gene nor Charles thought much of Mr. Monroe, but they knew they could not stand in their daughter's way. Jeannette married Blaine in February of 1909 and moved to his home in Warren, Pennsylvania. Two years later, Gene's first grandchild, a girl named Jeannette after her mother, was born.

By this time, the town of Geneva had grown by leaps and bounds. Lumber companies were harvesting Limberlost Swamp's tall trees to make such things as ship masts and furniture. Fuel companies continued to dig oil wells, and farmers were draining the wetlands to create more tillable land for crops. Gradually Gene and other area residents began to see that there was a dark side to all this progress. The development was destroying the natural environment and choking out the wildlife, and there was nothing anyone could do about it. Leaders as well as citizens in the early twentieth century had only the dimmest idea of what conservation was and why it was important, so there were few, if any, environmental-protection laws on the books.

Gene realized that she could no longer find many birds to photograph because the trees where they built their nests were gone. The moths and butterflies were gone, too, because their favorite plants and flowers had been plowed over. Although she hated to face the truth, it became clear to Gene that she could not continue her nature studies and photography at Limberlost.

In 1912, to get bird pictures for her next book, Gene went back to Sylvan Lake at Rome City, her favorite nature retreat from her youth and the place where she had met her husband. She bought a little cottage there and spent the summer taking pictures and writing. She also began looking around for a new property with plenty of natural areas for her to do her work in.

Later that summer she found a place, right on the lake, surrounded by woods and fields of wildflowers. With the money she earned from her books, Gene bought the property and designed the house she wanted. While it was under construction, Gene started on the landscaping. She collected wildflowers from all over the region and transplanted them in her yard. She hoped to acquire and plant a sample of every wild plant that grew in Indiana. All the time Gene was at the lake, Charles stayed in Geneva to attend to his businesses, usually visiting Gene on weekends.

In February 1914 the new house was finally ready to move into. Gene dubbed her new estate "Wildflower Woods." The house was bigger and nicer than Limberlost Cabin and included a darkroom and plenty of work space for Gene.

Later that year, Jeannette's second daughter arrived. The baby was named for her grandmother, Gene Stratton Monroe. During the first summer at Wildflower Woods, Jeannette brought the children there for an extended visit. Later that year, around Christmastime, Gene received word that her estranged brother Lemon was dying. She rushed to his side and was with him in his final days. Lemon's widow (his third wife) refused to take care of her late husband's twelve-year-old daughter, Leah Mary, so Gene took her in.

In 1916 Gene decided to buy a house in Fort Wayne for Jeannette and her family. Jeannette's husband, Blaine Monroe, was struggling financially, and the marriage was suffering too. Nevertheless, the Monroes would stay together four more years.

In 1917 Gene's book *Freckles* was made into a silent movie by Paramount Pictures in Hollywood. Gene was unhappy with the result—she felt that the film did not follow the novel or send the optimistic message she wanted to send. She resolved not to sell any more of her books to Hollywood unless she could have more control over the production.

By the fall of 1918, Gene was exhausted. She worked constantly, ate many meals on the run, and in general did not take good care of herself. It was clear that she needed a rest, so she checked herself into a hot-springs health clinic in upstate New York. After a month there, she was feeling much better. Unfortunately, she would not feel well for long. Throughout 1918, a severe flu epidemic had been sickening and killing people all over the world, and that winter, Gene caught it too. She was lucky to survive the often deadly illness, and it took her a long time to get over it.

The following spring, still feeling weak, Gene decided to move to a warmer climate. Several of her relatives lived in California, so she chose to go there. She sold most of her property in Indiana, including Limberlost, and moved into a small cottage in Los Angeles. She kept Wildflower Woods, however, planning to spend her summers there. Still involved in his Geneva businesses, Charles remained in Indiana.

Gene had not been in California long when Jeannette called to say her marriage was over. Her divorce was granted in October

1920, and afterward Jeannette and her two little girls moved to Los Angeles to live with Gene, who immediately bought a bigger house to accommodate them. Throughout this period, Gene continued to write, publishing nature books and articles, a women's column in *McCall's* magazine, at least one new novel, and even some poetry.

By 1923 Gene had decided to stay in California permanently and give up Wildflower Woods. She offered to donate the property to the state of Indiana for a state park and wildlife preserve. State officials did not respond, however, and Wildflower Woods would end up going to Jeannette after Gene's death. Finally, in the early 1940s, Jeannette would sell the place to the Gene Stratton-Porter Memorial Association, which in turn would donate it to the state. Today the Indiana State Museum system operates Wildflower Woods as a nature preserve and public museum.

While living in California, Gene published several more books and articles. She also began giving talks to various nature organizations and women's groups. At the same time, she was at work planning and overseeing the construction of two new houses, a main home and workshop in Bel Air and a vacation home on Catalina Island. As busy as she was, she remained interested in expanding her horizons with new projects. In spite of her negative experience with the *Freckles* film, the movie business still intrigued her.

In Los Angeles, Gene met many people in the motion picture industry, including a clean-cut filmmaker named Thomas Ince. Impressed with Ince's commitment to producing wholesome films, she discussed with him the possibility of making a movie from her novel *Michael O'Halloran*. Gene agreed to allow Ince to produce the film as long as she had control over how it was done. It was also agreed that Jeannette would write the screenplay. The chosen director was a young man named James Leo Meehan. Gene immediately hit it off with Leo (he went by his middle name), as did Jeannette.

The making of the silent film *Michael O'Halloran* was a rewarding enterprise in more ways than one. Upon its release in 1923, the movie was a success. In the meantime, Jeannette's working relationship with Leo Meehan had blossomed into romance. She and Leo married in June 1923. By then, Gene had begun to contemplate starting her own movie-production company. In the early 1920s, in partnership with her new son-in-law, she launched Gene Stratton-Porter Productions and began work on the silent-film version of her most popular novel, *Girl of the Limberlost*. Released that summer, the movie was a hit. Also premiering that summer was James Meehan, Jr., Gene's third grandchild and first grandson.

It is undoubtedly tragic that Gene Stratton-Porter died at the height of her success and happiness. On December 6, 1924, Gene's car was struck by a streetcar in downtown Los Angeles. She was rushed to the hospital, where she passed away about two hours later. She was sixty-one years old. Although Gene had expressed her wish to be buried under a tree, she was instead interred in a marble crypt in Hollywood Memorial Park Cemetery.

Most of the books and articles Gene had written in the months before her death were published posthumously, and Leo Meehan continued to run Gene Stratton-Porter Productions, producing five more films from Gene's novels. Later in the twentieth century, several of her works were made into movies by other film companies.

Decades after Gene's death, in 1999, her grandsons, James and John Meehan (the latter born a few years after Gene's death), had her remains removed and reburied at Wildflower Woods, under a magnificent oak tree. They also reburied the remains of their mother, Jeannette, who died in 1977 at age ninety, at Wildflower Woods.

Like Wildflower Woods, Limberlost eventually became a nature preserve. Thanks to Indiana's Wetlands Conservation Plan, approved in 1996, Limberlost Swamp has been partially restored. Limberlost Cabin, near Geneva, is preserved as an Indiana State Historic Site. In 2009 Gene was inducted into the Indiana Conservation Hall of Fame for her efforts to educate the public about environmental protection.

Many years ago, Geneve Stratton's father told her that he would rather see his child write a book he could be proud of than to see her sit on the throne of England. It's likely that Gene Stratton-Porter's books would have made her dad proud, especially her nature books. But more than that, with her writing and her conservation work, this talented, dedicated native Hoosier made the entire state of Indiana very proud indeed.

Overbeck sisters (left to right): Harriet (1872–1951), Margaret (1863–1911), Hannah (1870–1931), Elizabeth (1875–1936), Ida (1861–1946), and Mary Frances (1878–1955). Picture taken circa 1900. —Courtesy Overbeck Museum

THE OVERBECK SISTERS:
MARGARET, HANNAH, ELIZABETH, AND MARY FRANCES

Pottery Artists

A student seeking art instruction in Indiana in the early 1920s may have answered an ad that said: "Overbeck School of Pottery, Overbeck Studios. Founded 1911. Original designs and decorations. Designing, pottery making on wheel or hand built, and firing. Summer only: four weeks. Tuition, $35."

This student had probably heard of the Overbeck sisters, renowned art teachers and award-winning ceramic artists, and found the idea of taking pottery classes with them a thrilling prospect. To reach the home and studio of the Overbecks, where they held the classes, our aspiring potter might arrive in downtown Cambridge City and walk a few blocks to the two-story green clapboard house at the edge of town, with its neat shutters and colorful flower gardens. She would know it was the right house because of the ceramic sign, posted by the front gate, that bore the Overbeck monogram, OBK—this was the insignia that marked the bottom of all the sisters' beautiful pots, vases, bowls, tea sets, and figurines.

Following a walkway of handmade, rose-colored ceramic tiles to the front door, our eager art student may have been greeted by Harriet Overbeck, the sister who acted as the main hostess and housekeeper in the home. Harriet, serious but welcoming, would likely have led the visitor into the home's light-filled parlor, offered her a cup of tea, and asked her to sign the guest book. Among the names on those pages were those of artists, teachers, writers, and many others, from all parts of the globe.

Looking around, our student would have observed the simple but beautifully crafted cherry and walnut furniture—made long ago by the sisters' late father, John—offset by the ladies' own colorful paintings on the walls and ceramic pieces displayed on every table and shelf. On the floor were braided rugs crafted by the artists' late mother, Sarah. The sisters' original family name was Overpeck, but a few years after John and Sarah's deaths, the siblings changed their name to Overbeck.

Finally, the prospective student would meet her teachers, Elizabeth, Hannah, and Mary, all, like Harriet, dark-haired and simply dressed. After the arrangements were made, four weeks of hard work would begin.

———

In 1868 John and Sarah Overpeck moved from Ohio to a farm north of the thriving town of Cambridge City, Indiana. At the time, the couple had two daughters, Ida, born in 1861, and Margaret, born two years later. The Overpecks settled into their farmhouse, where six more children were born. Hannah came along in 1870, then Harriet in 1872. Another girl, born in 1873, died in infancy. Elizabeth arrived in 1875, and Mary Frances followed three years later. The last child was Charles, the only boy; born in 1881, he was twenty years younger than his eldest sister. In 1883 the family moved into a large house in town; this would be the home of Margaret, Hannah, Elizabeth, and Mary Overbeck for the rest of their lives.

John Overpeck had become a farmer by necessity (how else to feed such a large brood in those days?), but he also earned income as a carpenter. His passion was woodworking, and he was a master craftsman. Both he and his wife were educated and cultured, and they encouraged their children to pursue the arts. John taught his daughters as well as his son to work with wood, metal, clay, and other materials. His wife, Sarah Borger Overpeck, was highly skilled at needlework, knitting, quilting, rug braiding, and tatting (lace making). She also painted, a pursuit she urged her daughters to share in. As parents, John and Sarah were unusual, not only in ensuring that their daughters were well educated, but also in hoping their girls would never marry, preferring that they focus on developing their talents and fulfilling their artistic potential.

The Overpeck children all attended public school in Cambridge City, and eventually all but Ida went to college. They were also taught various crafts by their parents, and as they grew older, the siblings tutored one another as well. In 1890, Ida, the eldest, opened a photography studio in town, assisted for a time by her sister Hannah. Shortly afterward, however, Hannah left to go to teachers' college (then called "normal school"); later, Mary would attend the same college, Indiana State Normal School. After graduating, they both taught school for a time. Mary first taught in Boulder, Colorado, but later she came back to Indiana and taught in Cambridge City and in the nearby town of Centerville. Hannah taught for only one year, in Clinton, Indiana, before she became too ill to continue. She suffered from neuritis, a progressive nerve disease that would eventually make her an invalid.

Margaret entered the Art Academy of Cincinnati in 1892, followed by Hannah and Mary; later, Margaret and Mary would also study art at Columbia University in New York and at the Ipswich Summer Art School in Massachusetts. For a long time, Margaret worked as a college art instructor, including eleven years at DePauw University in Greencastle, Indiana, before returning to Cambridge City in 1910. As a painter, she was especially good at portraits, able to capture her subjects' personalities. She was also an excellent teacher—each of her student's artwork looked different, meaning that Margaret brought out her students' individual talents rather than teaching them to copy her style.

Elizabeth was the only Overbeck to be formally trained in pottery, attending the College for Clayworking and Ceramics in Alfred, New York. This technical education would prove invaluable as the sisters' pottery studio evolved. Harriet studied not art but music, becoming an accomplished vocalist, pianist, and violinist. She received classical music training in Chicago, Cincinnati, and Leipzig, Germany. She also spoke several languages. Charles became an engineer.

In 1893 Ida upset the family when she married a local wheelwright and woodcarver named Martin Funk and closed her photography studio. The couple never had children, and as far as is known, Ida did not pursue her photographic ambitions after her marriage. None of the other Overbeck women would ever marry, though Charles would, eventually giving his sisters a beloved niece and nephew.

By about 1903, the four artist sisters had developed a special interest in designing patterns for ceramics and pottery. They began entering—and winning—design contests in *Keramic Studio* magazine, a popular periodical for people interested in china painting, which was a common hobby among women in those days. Soon afterward, the Overbecks started displaying their paintings, drawings, and early pottery at various art exhibitions in Indiana and elsewhere.

John Overpeck died in 1904, and Sarah passed away two years later. By this time all of their children were grown, and most were working or in school. By 1910, all but Ida and Charles had returned home to live in the big house they'd grown up in. Mary was already living at home, teaching in a local school. Harriet had come home, too, and was giving music and language lessons for income. She also conducted local choirs and orchestras. Elizabeth returned from ceramics school in New York state in the late spring of 1910. Hannah was also home, having given up teaching after only one year because of her neuritis. Sadly, Margaret, too, was unwell. She had been hit by a car in Chicago in 1907 and incurred serious head injuries. She partly recovered, but by 1910 she had become too weak to continue teaching, and she came back to Cambridge City.

Living together, the sisters helped one another develop their art. Margaret, having the most experience, took the lead in teaching the others and encouraging their artistic experiments. It was Margaret who suggested the sisters open a pottery studio of their own. Her idea was to earn a living selling their artwork. For extra money, the sisters would also teach ceramics classes. Harriet, too, would contribute to the family income by giving music lessons.

Margaret laid down a few artistic rules for the pottery undertaking: 1. The shape of each piece must be carefully planned before it was created, and anything that did not turn out perfectly was to be destroyed; 2. each item must be unique and hand crafted so that, in contrast to the identical pieces produced in pottery factories, nothing would be an exact copy; and 3. the designs should always be based on nature and should never be "borrowed" from other artists' designs. Originality was paramount. One of Margaret's mottos was "Borrowed art is bad art." Elizabeth added this idea: the decoration on an object should accentuate its shape. A tall, thin vase should be decorated with long, vertical patterns, while a short, round bowl should have soft, round, horizontal decorations.

Agreeing on these principles, the four potting sisters, with help from Harriet, who was not a potter, began preparing their studio. The main workshop was in the basement, where the electric potter's wheel was kept and the heavy work of mixing and preparing clay was done. A kerosene-fueled kiln was built in the backyard for firing the pottery. A back room became their design studio, and the front room served as a showroom for buyers. Classes would be held in the studio and workshop. The Overbeck sisters never expected to get rich by making art pottery, but they felt that between selling pottery, teaching classes, and perhaps getting an occasional commission for a special piece, they could get by.

The Overbeck Pottery was ready to open in the spring of 1911. The sisters had barely begun their first projects, however, when in August, Margaret died of complications from her accident four years before. Though grief-stricken, the other sisters forged ahead with the pottery studio, always honoring Margaret's vision and following her rules.

While they were determined, the sisters did worry about several things when they started their pottery business. For one thing, they were uncertain if they were strong enough for the physical work such as digging up clay and carrying it to the workshop, as well as rolling out the clay by hand to get the right consistency, which required some muscle. They also worried about being able to take care of the equipment. If the electric potter's wheel broke down, they would have to fix it themselves. And there was the kiln, fueled by kerosene that was kept in a tank in a back room. Kerosene was dangerously flammable (not to mention smelly).

In addition, the Overbecks were concerned about running the business aspects of the pottery, as none of the sisters had business experience, and they worried about whether they could make enough money to live on. They weren't sure their work would even be taken seriously, as women artists were often dismissed as being incapable of creating true art.

In spite of these concerns, the sisters did not waver from their goal. They divided the work according to each sister's best skills. Hannah was the main designer of the items' shapes and decorations. She based many of her designs on the plants, birds, and insects in her own yard. A perfectionist, she always wanted to get every detail right.

Elizabeth was the technician, creating the clay mixtures and the glazes. Often, she was also the one who made the pottery itself, usually forming it on a potter's wheel but later doing more and more by hand, coiling ropes of clay into the desired shape and refining the surface with her fingers. Some potters purposely leave finger marks on the surface of the finished piece, so people can tell it was handmade, but Elizabeth liked to make her pottery as smooth and perfect as possible. Once the clay piece was formed, it was then baked, or "fired," in the kiln to make it hard. Elizabeth did most of the firing, as neither Hannah nor Mary liked dealing with the kiln. The item would then be decorated with color glazes and fired again to set the glaze, making it glossy and waterproof. Elizabeth experimented for years with glazes of different colors and shininess, and she was considered a great innovator in that regard.

Once the clay item was fired the first time, Mary did most of the decorating, usually based on Hannah's designs, and the glazing, using the glazes that Elizabeth created. Glazes are tricky. For one thing, the potter can't always see where the glaze is going as she brushes it on. Furthermore, glazes often turn a different color when the piece is fired, so it is hard to know what the final color will look like. After the item was decorated and glazed, it would be given back to Elizabeth for the second firing.

While the sisters often divided the work of pottery making this way, at times they switched tasks. Mary would frequently create a design instead of Hannah; both Mary and Hannah sometimes worked with the clay, like Elizabeth (though only Elizabeth used the potter's wheel); and Elizabeth might do her own glazing. Although the sisters occasionally used molds to make cups and saucers in dish sets, for consistency, the finishing and decorating was always done by hand. Besides pottery, Hannah and Mary created paintings, printed bookplates, worked with fabrics, made jewelry, and even built furniture. They sold some of these things for extra money, while others they kept for their home or to give as gifts.

For her part, Harriet supported her sisters' efforts by taking care of the housework. She also inspired them by playing the piano or violin while they worked. In addition, she added to the household income with her private lessons in music and foreign languages. For all her musical and linguistic talent, however, she felt different from her sisters because she did not paint or make pottery. Acquaintances said she was oversensitive and "very much out of place in Cambridge City."

Although the Overbecks were generally well-liked, some people in town thought it was odd that they never married and still lived together at their family home. But the sisters didn't care—they never wanted to be like everyone else. Later, as they became famous, folks wondered why they turned down opportunities to make a lot of money. But they felt that they did not need a lot of money. They lived very frugally, growing their own vegetables and raising chickens for eggs and meat. They sewed their own clothes and even built furniture. They also made decorations for the house and created their own Christmas cards. Once, one of the sisters was told she needed dentures, but they were expensive so she made a set herself!

In November 1913 the Overbeck sisters learned that their brother, Charles, had died of a lingering illness, leaving a wife and two young children, Virgina, age two, and Charles Jr., an infant. Later, the sisters took care of the children for two summers while their mother, Hallie, attended summer classes to become a teacher. Mary, in particular, doted on her niece and nephew, making them toys and reading to them every day. This is not surprising, as Mary was the playful one. When she wasn't working on one of the sisters' collaborative pieces, she liked to make small, hand-sculpted clay figurines of people and animals. Children, in particular, loved the little sculptures.

At first Mary made the figurines just for fun. She would fashion four- or five-inch clay figures of animals or of people she knew around town just to use up leftover clay or try out a new glaze color for Elizabeth. Sometimes the sisters would put them out on their "bargain table," and they became popular items. Before long, Mary began making them in earnest.

One day, their young nephew, Charles, made his own miniature animal of clay. It was not like any real animal, just something from his imagination. The sisters put his funny little creature into the kiln with their next batch of pottery. Visitors to the studio noticed Charles's curious little sculpture and asked about it. This gave the sisters the idea to make more such whimsical creatures, which they called "grotesques" because they were so strange-looking. Elizabeth called them "the humor of the kiln." Mary was the one who loved creating these grotesques, and they sold very well. When customers came to the studio to buy dishes or vases, their children always wanted one of Mary's comical little figurines. Sometimes the sisters made more money from the grotesques than from their serious pottery.

Mary continued to create more realistic figurines as well. Some were likenesses of historical figures such as George Washington or Abraham Lincoln, while others represented a common character like a doctor or a bartender. People began paying her to create figurines of their loved ones or family pets.

At the height of the sisters' success in the 1920s, the biggest department store in Indianapolis, L. S. Ayres, sold Overbeck tea sets and vases. They were advertised as one-of-a-kind, handmade items. But the pottery became so popular that the store wanted the Overbecks to produce much more, much faster. Marshall Field, a huge store in Chicago, also wanted Overbeck products. At one point, each of these stores offered the sisters a lot of money if they would accelerate their production to a certain number of items each year. To make that many pieces, the sisters would have to use molds for everything and take other shortcuts to produce a lot of dishes and vases quickly. But that would mean the things they made would be copies, not unique objects of art. Doing this would go against the rules that the sisters had agreed to when they started the pottery business.

It was hard to decide. They could make a lot of money, which, in spite of their thrifty ways, they needed. Some of the materials they used for their pottery and paintings were expensive, and their funds often ran short. But if they accepted a contract, they would be giving up the ideals they had learned from their sister Margaret about being real artists. In the end, they turned down the deals.

Hannah, who had been ill from her neuritis since she finished college, got worse. By 1925 the pain was so bad that it hurt her to move. Her sisters hired a man to build a small rope-and-pulley elevator so she wouldn't have to walk up and down the stairs. She often had to be carried from place to place around the house. Hannah still loved to draw, however, even when her hands hurt. Whenever she wanted to draw, her sisters would bring her a pad of paper and put the pencil in her fingers for her. Hannah continued to design pottery this way for several years.

During the first twenty or so years of the Overbecks' pottery business, the town of Cambridge City was a busy place with many wealthy visitors, and the money flowed. This is not to say the Overbeck sisters were becoming wealthy, but they earned a comfortable living from selling their pottery and giving art lessons. Their reputation grew as they entered exhibitions and won awards in Indiana as well as Chicago, Cincinnati, San Francisco, and elsewhere. Travelers liked to stop at the Overbeck home to see how the pottery was made, as did reporters from magazines and newspapers, making the Overbeck name even more famous.

After the Great Depression began in 1929, however, it was a different story. Few people could afford to travel, so Cambridge City had fewer visitors. Likewise, folks stopped spending on extras like art lessons, not to mention art itself. Even people who had money were afraid to spend it on art, in case times got worse.

The sisters worked together to get through the bad times. When they ran out of cash, Elizabeth and Mary walked downtown on Saturdays, when people were shopping, with a basket of their little figurines, selling them to folks on the street. Figures of well-known personalities around town were especially popular.

In 1930 Mary, who always enjoyed children, undertook a special project of her own for the local library—a detailed model of a Spanish sailing ship for young library visitors to play with. The thirty-six-inch-long ship, which Mary named the *Don Quixote* (key-HO-tay) after the hero of a famous Spanish story, contained thirty-two brightly colored little ceramic pirates, which the children could move around. The ship is still on display at the Cambridge City Public Library, now encased in glass in its Museum of Overbeck Pottery downstairs.

In 1931, as the national economy grew worse, Hannah died. Only Elizabeth and Mary were left to run the studio. The two now had to create their own pottery designs, some of which they based on their late sister's sketches. They continued to produce beautiful work and to enter art competitions, and they continued to win awards.

In 1933 Chicago held its Century of Progress International Exposition, a huge event to celebrate the city's one hundredth anniversary. The Overbecks submitted a tea set for entry in the Fine Arts Division of this extremely competitive nationwide contest. It won first prize. Afterward, the Marshall Field company displayed the set in its store as the winning artwork. This visibility brought the Overbeck sisters more attention and more commissioned work.

After Franklin D. Roosevelt became president in 1933, he began an ambitious project to stimulate an economic recovery. Known as

These vases, decorated with a design called "Hills and Horses," were among the Overbeck sisters' best-known works. —Courtesy Overbeck Museum

the New Deal, part of the plan was for the federal government to pay laborers to build roads, bridges, parks, and trails throughout the country. One of these New Deal programs, called the Public Works Administration (PWA), also hired artists to produce public artwork and exhibits. The Overbeck sisters were lucky enough to be offered a PWA contract. One project they made was a pair of large aqua-and-white vases. The design, called "Horses and Hills," showed little ponies galloping over rows and rows of hills.

By then the Overbecks' work was so well known that in 1936, Indiana art collector John Nixon hired them to make a sculpture for President Franklin Roosevelt and First Lady Eleanor Roosevelt—a life-size ceramic rooster. Another admirer asked them to make a little grouping of figurines for Mrs. Roosevelt; it portrayed George and Martha Washington sitting at a table with their dog at their feet. The sisters also created a gorgeous tea set for Mrs. Roosevelt as a personal gift from them.

In December 1936, Elizabeth died, leaving Mary, age fifty-eight, as the last of potters. Harriet was overcome with sadness, saying, "The real light of the household has gone out." The following year, Ida's husband, Martin Funk, died, and Ida moved back into the Overbeck family home with her sisters. This may have made the place less lonely, but like Harriet, Ida was not a potter, so it was up to Mary to carry on by herself making pottery under the Overbeck name.

In 1941, Harriet moved to Cincinnati, where she remained until her death ten years later. Ida died in 1946. Mary, living all alone, continued to make vases and dishes as special orders, using Elizabeth's special glazes, whose secret formulas Mary never revealed. She also continued to create figurines and grotesques to suit herself. It always made her happy to go into the library and see

Mary Frances Overbeck at work, circa 1950. —Courtesy Overbeck Museum

children playing with the *Don Quixote* and its pirates. When Mary died in 1955, the Overbeck Pottery studio closed for good.

Today the Overbeck home is privately owned, but visits can be arranged by appointment. The house was added to the National Register of Historic Places in 1976. A nearby historical marker explains the building's significance. At the other end of town, on the lower level of the Cambridge City Public Library, is the Overbeck Museum, where much of the sisters' work can be seen.

Through good times and bad, the Overbeck sisters faced their professional and personal challenges and addressed them one by one, working together under a shared vision of living independently and creating genuine art. They lived and worked on their own terms, finally proving to themselves—and the world—that women can indeed be true artists.

Portrait of Madam Walker (1867–1919), taken in 1914
—Courtesy A'Lelia Bundles, Walker family collection

MADAM
C. J. WALKER

*Entrepreneur and
Philanthropist*

The story of Sarah Breedlove, better known as Madam C. J. Walker, is a phenomenal one. Born to former slaves and raised in wretched poverty, she worked incredibly hard to make a better life for herself and her daughter, eventually becoming one of the wealthiest black women in America. Rarely has a person started with so little and ended up with so much through her own efforts, using her natural intelligence, steely determination, and willingness to work, work, work.

Sarah Breedlove was born on a cotton plantation in Delta, Louisiana, on December 23, 1867—only five years after Abraham Lincoln ended slavery with the Emancipation Proclamation. She was the first person in her family to be born free. Her parents, Owen and Minerva Breedlove, had both been slaves on the Burney Plantation, as had her older sister and brothers.

After the Emancipation Proclamation, the Breedloves' former master, Robert Burney, allowed the Breedlove family to stay in their ramshackle one-room cabin and keep working in the fields as sharecroppers, meaning the Breedloves could farm their own cotton but had to share the profits with Mr. Burney, who still owned the

119

land. In practice, after paying Mr. Burney for the cottonseeds and the use of his land and equipment, the profits never quite covered what Mr. Burney said the Breedloves owed him. Thus, like nearly all sharecroppers in the post–Civil War South, no matter how hard they worked, the Breedloves were always penniless and in debt. Minerva took in laundry, assisted by her older daughter, Louvenia, for a little extra money, but the family still struggled to keep food on the table.

Sarah, who was sometimes called "Winnie" as a child, was the fifth of six children. Besides her older sister, Louvenia, Sarah had three older brothers—Owen Jr., Alexander (Alex), and James. A younger brother, Solomon, was born about a year after Sarah. Everyone in the family worked as soon as they were old enough to walk. At age three, Sarah began helping in the fields, poking holes in the soil with a stick and dropping in the cottonseeds. By age six, she was out picking cotton in the hot Louisiana sun. She also helped her mother and sister with the laundry, which required dunking the clothes in soapy boiling water, fishing them out with a long stick, scrubbing them against a washboard, rinsing them out, squeezing out the excess water, and hanging them up on a clothesline to dry before ironing and folding them. With all the work to do on the plantation, Sarah never went to school.

When Sarah was about six years old, her mother died, perhaps of cholera or malaria, both widespread diseases at the time. Owen Breedlove tried to keep his family together, but about two years later, he too died, possibly of smallpox or one of the other diseases that were rampant among the poor in those days. By that time, Louvenia, who was about fourteen years older than Sarah, had married a man named Jesse Powell and later had a baby boy, whom the couple named Willie.

After their parents' deaths, the Breedlove children could not keep the plantation going on their own, and they lost their home. After that, around 1877, Alex Breedlove moved to the town of Vicksburg, Mississippi, just across the Mississippi River from Delta, to look for a job. He found work at a grocery store. About a year later, Louvenia and Jesse took Sarah, now age ten, to live in Vicksburg as well. The girls took in laundry, while Jesse most likely worked as a day laborer.

In Vicksburg, Louvenia and Sarah spent all day with their arms in big washtubs, their hands and arms always cracked and sore from the strong soap they used. Sarah didn't mind working hard—she'd never known any other kind of life—but Louvenia's husband, Jesse, was a mean and abusive man with a violent temper; Sarah later described him as "cruel." Yet she had nowhere else to go.

About three years after Sarah, Louvenia, and Jesse went to Vicksburg, Alex Breedlove moved to St. Louis, Missouri, where he found work and eventually became a barber. A year or two later, Owen Jr. and James joined Alex in St. Louis, and the three brothers opened a barbershop of their own. Not long afterward, Owen would leave for the West while the youngest Breedlove, Solomon, would move to St. Louis to join his brothers at the barbershop.

Meanwhile back in Vicksburg, Sarah, unable to stand the way Jesse treated her, found a way out. In 1882, when she was fourteen, she met a man named Moses McWilliams, possibly at church. Little is known about Moses or what his occupation was. All that can be assumed is that he must have been kinder to Sarah than Jesse was because when he asked her to marry him, she said yes. Sarah claimed that she married Moses in order to get a home of her own. After the marriage, Sarah continued to take in laundry for income; both she and Moses may also have worked seasonally in the cotton fields around Vicksburg.

Three years later, in June 1885, Sarah was overjoyed to give birth to a daughter. She and Moses named the baby Lelia. But when Lelia was about three years old, Moses died. The cause of his death is unknown. Now Sarah, age twenty, was a widow with a little girl to raise. She certainly did not want to move in with Louvenia and Jesse again, so she decided to join her brothers in St. Louis.

Upon their arrival in St. Louis, Sarah and Lelia probably stayed with one of Sarah's brothers, at least for a time, and Sarah went back to doing laundry. Shortly after settling in, Sarah joined St. Paul's AME Church, a black church in the neighborhood. St. Paul's welcomed well-to-do African Americans and poor ones alike. The church members helped one another through difficult times, and Sarah felt supported there. She became special friends with a former schoolteacher named Jessie Robinson, who would later work for Sarah for a while. Jessie, the middle-class wife of newspaper publisher C. K. Robinson, taught Sarah the importance of presenting herself nicely, with careful grooming, proper manners, and good diction. She also got Sarah involved in community activities and helping the less fortunate. All of this helped Sarah gain confidence. Jessie and Sarah stayed in touch for many years, even after Sarah moved away from St. Louis.

When Lelia was old enough, Sarah enrolled her in the local public school for black children (in those days, most schools were segregated—that is, students were separated by race). Sarah wanted to be sure her daughter had the education she herself had never received. Lelia seemed to like school, and she was a good student.

In April of 1893, Sarah and her family were grief-stricken at the sudden death of Alex, who passed away from an intestinal illness. About a year later, Sarah married a man named John Davis. On the marriage certificate, Sarah's first name appears as Sallie, apparently a nickname she went by in St. Louis. Sarah married John thinking that he could give Lelia, now nine years old, a better life in a good home. But he turned out to be a bad husband. He drank too much, he was violent, and he even ran around with other women. Furthermore, it seemed he could not hold on to a job for long—various records showed him as a laundry worker, a porter, and a janitor. Whatever his job, his income was not much, and Sarah continued to take in laundry to make ends meet.

At home, Sarah and John fought bitterly. The situation was so upsetting to Lelia that she started missing school, and her grades fell. Sarah began saving up money so that when Lelia finished elementary school, she could send her to a good private boarding school for black students. Although she would miss her daughter, Sarah hoped that Lelia would do better away from home, in a healthier environment. Besides the conflicts at home, the family's neighborhood in St. Louis was full of crime and indecency. When the time came, in 1902, Sarah chose Knoxville College, a well-respected African American high school and college in Knoxville, Tennessee, for Lelia.

While Lelia was away at school, more tragedies befell the Breedloves. In November 1902, Sarah's brother James died of heart disease, and only nine months later, Solomon, the youngest Breedlove, died of tuberculosis. Later in 1903 Sarah and John Davis separated, and John moved in with his girlfriend. It was a lot for Sarah to go through, but she devoted herself to her church and charity work. Through her church activities, she developed a new self-confidence as she worked with different people and learned leadership skills. She even began speaking in front of groups. Soon Sarah started thinking about her future. As she later recalled:

> I was at my washtubs one morning with a heavy wash before me. As I bent over the washboard, and looked at my arms buried in soapsuds, I said to myself: "What are you going to do when you grow old and your back gets stiff? Who is going to take care of your little girl?" This set me to thinking, but with all my thinking I couldn't see how I, a poor washerwoman, was going to better my condition.

At age thirty-four, Sarah barely knew how to read and write. She knew she would not get very far without more education, so she signed up for night classes at the local public school. She still washed clothes all day, but now she attended school several evenings a week. There she discovered a passion for learning that would last the rest of her life.

Shortly after John left her, Sarah had a new man in her life—Charles Joseph Walker. Charles, who went by C.J., was charming, nicely dressed, and relatively well educated, and he had a good job selling subscriptions and ads for one of the black newspapers in St. Louis. He and Sarah began dating.

Despite these promising new beginnings, Sarah's self-confidence was undercut by a problem with her hair. Although she had always worn fresh, clean, and neatly pressed clothes—at least partly to show off how good her laundry service was—her hair was becoming increasingly dry, brittle, and patchy. She often wore head wraps to cover her bald spots. Hair and scalp problems were common among poor women, who usually suffered from poor diets, inadequate health care, and constant stress. Treatments that were meant to groom the hair of black women often contained harsh ingredients and frequently did more harm than good. Sarah tried numerous different hair products, but nothing helped. Nothing, that is, until she met the woman who would change not only her hair but her whole life—Annie Turnbo.

Originally from Illinois, Annie had developed a shampoo for African American women that claimed to restore the hair and scalp to radiant health, allowing the hair to grow in thickly, even in the bald spots. Later, she developed other hair-care products, which she sold door-to-door in black neighborhoods. Annie came to St. Louis in 1902 hoping to expand her business. Her first step was to open a small salon and advertise her products and services. The next was to hire and train sales agents to allow her to cover more ground and sell more products. Later she started selling her products by mail order as well.

When Sarah used Annie's products, she liked them. Soon, probably in 1903, she became a sales agent for Annie's company. Little did Annie know that her new sales representative would soon become her biggest competitor.

In working for Annie, Sarah learned about hair-care products and sales techniques, which she would eventually replicate for her own business. Sarah earned better money selling Annie's hair products than she did washing clothes, though she continued to do both, saving money for the future.

Meanwhile, Sarah's last surviving brother, Owen Jr., who had left St. Louis for Albuquerque, New Mexico, in 1883, disappeared around 1900, leaving a wife named Lucy and four young daughters. It's unknown whether he died or simply left. After Owen was gone, Lucy moved with her little girls to Denver, Colorado, where she took in boarders and did laundry to support herself and her children. In

1905 Sarah decided to leave St. Louis and join her sister-in-law out West, where she planned to sell Annie Turnbo's products to a new market in Denver, figuring there would be less competition in the younger city.

Sarah, now thirty-seven years old, left for Denver in July. She moved in with Lucy and her girls—Anjetta, fifteen; Thirsapen, thirteen; Mattie, eight; and Gladis, five—and took a job as a cook in a rooming house, selling Annie Turnbo's hair products in her spare time.

Not long after she began working for Annie, Sarah got the idea of creating her own hair products and starting her own business. She began experimenting with different mixtures shortly after arriving in Denver, no doubt using Annie's products as a starting point then adding and subtracting ingredients by trial and error. She may have had some previous knowledge of hair care gained from her barber brothers, and some historians believe she consulted E. L. Scholtz, a pharmacist she had once worked for, asking him to analyze the ingredients in Annie's products and perhaps urging him to suggest others. She said that she tried out various blends on her own hair and on friends and family members until she had perfected the formula.

Years later, when people asked Sarah how she came up with her hair-growing treatment, she told a whimsical story full of exotic images that added to her product's mystique:

> One night I had a dream, and in that dream a big black man appeared to me and told me what to mix up for my hair. Some of the remedy was grown in Africa, but I sent for it, mixed it, put it on my scalp, and in a few weeks my hair was coming in faster than it had ever fallen out.
>
> I tried it on my friends; it helped them. I made up my mind to sell it.

About six months after Sarah moved to Denver, C. J. Walker, her boyfriend from St. Louis, joined her there. In January of 1906, they were married and moved into their own place. C.J., who had his own business interests in other areas, helped his bride launch her company and market her product line, beginning with its name.

Upon marrying C.J., Sarah became known as "Madam" C. J. Walker and her business was dubbed Madam C. J. Walker Manufacturing Company; Sarah felt that "Madam Walker" had more flair than "Sarah Walker" and gave her and her products both an air of authority and a feeling of European allure. C.J. himself always referred to his wife as "Madam."

Besides his name, C.J. gave Sarah business advice, helping her create newspaper ads to improve sales. She took his suggestion to heart, spending every spare dime on advertisements. The ads would bring in mail orders, but first Madam needed to show women how well her products worked. Like Annie Turnbo, she began by going door-to-door with her products and hair-care tools, giving hair treatments in her customers' homes, though she would soon open a salon of her own.

Madam's treatment, which she called "the Walker System," consisted of washing the customer's hair with her Vegetable Shampoo, then rubbing her Wonderful Hair Grower into the woman's scalp. Finally she applied her special hair oil, called Glossine, to make the hair softer and more manageable, combing it through with a special steel comb, which she heated on the stove; the heat helped the Glossine penetrate the hair and facilitated styling. For women with serious scalp conditions such as psoriasis (then called tetter), she also sold an ointment called Tetter Salve. After seeing the good results, the women nearly always bought more Walker products.

Madam was careful to say that her products were hair growers, not hair straighteners. They were created to promote healthy scalps and hair and to grow new hair, not to make black women's hair look a certain way. She made this distinction so that African American commentators would not criticize her for trying to make black women's hair look more like that of white women. Instead, she simply wanted to help African American women bring out their own natural beauty and feel more confident about their appearance.

As Madam began to see success with her hair products, she quit her job as a cook and took in laundry once again, so she could arrange her schedule around hair appointments. Shortly after the Walker Company was started, Lelia, now twenty-one and finished with school, joined her mother in Denver to help out with the new business. Madam had already enlisted her older nieces, Anjetta and Thirsapen, to mix and package the products, and to pack and ship the mail orders that soon began to pour in. It was not long before Sarah Breedlove Walker was finally able to leave her washtub behind for good.

C.J. remained a big help to his wife, but Madam Walker definitely had her own ideas about how to expand the business, whether C.J. agreed with them or not. Since there were not many African Americans living in Denver, Madam decided to start traveling to promote her products in other towns. C.J. thought she would be wasting too much time and money on travel, but Madam was convinced that she could increase her sales many times over by covering more ground. She was right.

Traveling by railroad, Madam visited many of the towns along the train route from Denver. In addition to going door-to-door to women's homes, she often arranged to speak to groups at various meeting places, where she demonstrated her products and technique. Within a year, she was training others in the Walker System and teaching them to sell Walker products. Once trained, these agents, whom Madam called "hair culturalists," would buy products from Madam and resell them to make money for themselves. In this way, Madam not only increased her own profits but also shared her business success with other black women, who otherwise would have to work in low-paying jobs, just as she had done. Her agents often wrote her letters telling her how working as a Walker hair culturalist had made their lives better, allowing them, for the first time in their lives, to earn enough money to live on. Helping other black women was a big part of Madam Walker's personal philosophy.

When Madam was on the road, Lelia stayed in Denver managing the salon that her mother had opened, while her cousins, Lucy's daughters Anjetta and Thirsapen, continued to make Walker products and ship them out. Within two years, the company was showing thousands of dollars in profits.

With every success, Madam started thinking about her next step. As she saw it, her company could expand nationwide. In 1908 she decided to open a new headquarters in a city with a larger African American population than Denver had. After visiting several cities, she chose Pittsburgh for her new operation, which included a beauty school that Madam named Lelia College of Beauty Culture. Closing up the Denver shop, Lelia moved to Pittsburgh to help manage the new headquarters and the school named for her. Not long afterward, she met a man named John Robinson and fell in love. In October of 1909, Lelia and John were married.

After two years in Pittsburgh, Madam went on a business trip to Indianapolis. She liked the city right away, and George Knox, publisher of the *Indianapolis Freeman*, one of the most respected African American newspapers in the country, encouraged her to move there. Being in the center of the country and the hub of several railroads, Indianapolis might well be a better place for her company headquarters than Pittsburgh, Madam thought. It would be easy to mail products from there and to go traveling in all directions. The city also had a thriving African American business community.

In 1910 Madam made the move to Indianapolis, established an office for the Madam C. J. Walker Company, and began running ads in the local black newspapers. Lelia remained in Pittsburgh, though her husband had left her after only a year of marriage, and she continued to run Lelia College. She would legally divorce John Robinson in 1914.

On one of her train trips, Sarah had met a young black college student who was working as a porter for the railroad. His name was F. B. (Freeman Briley) Ransom. As they talked, Madam saw that F.B. was a smart and serious young man, working his way through law school. Sarah told him to contact her when he graduated, saying she would give him a job. Sure enough, in Indianapolis, F.B. called her and said that he was now a lawyer, and Madam hired him to take care of her company's legal matters. It was one of the best decisions she ever made. F. B. Ransom later became the manager of the Walker Company's Indianapolis operations, and he did his job very well. He always gave Madam good advice, and he remained her close friend for the rest of her life. Whenever Madam set off on a business trip, she left F. B. Ransom in charge, keeping in close touch with him by mail.

After a while in Indianapolis, Madam bought a nice house and built a small factory and beauty salon in the back, and by 1911 she had built a second Lelia College. She hired many local people—mostly African Americans—to work for the company. One of these locals was a teenage girl named Fairy Mae Bryant. Mae (she went by her middle name) often visited her grandmother, who lived very near the Walker factory, and she began running errands for Madam and the other people working at the factory for a few coins. Noticing Mae's long, dark braids and intelligent manner, Madam took an interest in the girl, whose widowed mother was struggling to raise her and seven other children. Mae, who was of mixed racial heritage—African American, Native American, and European—had a striking face and beautiful waist-length hair. Madam thought she'd make a perfect model for Walker products.

When Lelia came to visit her mother in 1911, she, too, became intrigued by thirteen-year-old Mae Bryant. They developed a close relationship, and in 1912, having no children of her own, Lelia approached Mae's mother and asked if she might let her adopt Mae. She promised Mrs. Bryant that she could continue to see and write to her daughter any time. Understanding that Lelia could give Mae opportunities that she herself could never provide, Mrs. Bryant agreed. In October of 1912 Lelia Robinson became Mae's legal guardian and took her back to Pittsburgh as Mae Robinson. Later both Lelia and Mae would change their surname to Walker.

Madam was very happy to have the bright and lovely Mae as her granddaughter, and as the girl got older, Madam often took her along on business trips. Both Madam and Lelia hoped that Mae could take over the company someday, which she eventually did.

Although Madam Walker worked night and day, she did make time to enjoy herself in Indianapolis. She bought a couple of automobiles—still a novelty in the 1910s—attended social events, and entertained guests lavishly at her home. She also made time to help the community. Remembering how the women at St. Paul's Church in St. Louis, such as Jessie Robinson, had helped her and other people in need, she was now glad to have enough money to do more for the underprivileged, including giving Christmas turkeys and gift baskets to poor families in her neighborhood.

Madam Walker and friends at the dedication of the new YMCA building in Indianapolis, 1913. The man on the left is newspaper publisher George Knox; standing behind Madam is attorney F. B. Ransom; and the hatless man in the center is legendary educator and activist Booker T. Washington. —Courtesy A'Lelia Bundles, Walker family collection

In 1911 Madam Walker made her biggest gift yet, a donation that would bring her much recognition in Indianapolis. Hearing that the city's African American YMCA was in dire need of a new building, Madam Walker gave the organization $1,000—the largest donation they'd ever received from an African American woman. The newspapers wrote about Madam Walker and her generous gift, and black leaders across the nation began to know who she was. Her fame grew, and in 1913 she was invited to be a featured speaker at the National Negro Business League convention, where she told her story:

> I am a woman that came from the cotton fields of the South. I was promoted from there to the washtub. Then I was promoted to the cook kitchen, and from there I promoted myself into the business of manufacturing hair goods and preparations. . . . I have built my own factory on my own ground. . . . Now my object in life is not simply to make money for myself or to spend it on myself. . . . I love to use a part of what I make in trying to help others.

In the meantime, sadly, Madam and C.J.'s marriage had crumbled. In addition to their business disagreements, C.J. was drinking, and he had taken up with another woman. Madam had also heard that C.J. was stealing from the company. Finally, she had enough, and in August 1912 she divorced him, though she kept his name for business reasons.

Also in 1912, another important person joined the Walker Company. On an early business trip to Louisville, Kentucky, Madam Walker had met a teacher named Alice Kelly. When Alice's school closed two years later, Madam hired her to help run the Indianapolis factory. She trusted Alice so much that she gave her the secret formula for the Walker hair products, something only Lelia and Madam herself had been privy to before.

Alice Kelly did more for Madam Walker than work at the factory; she also served as Madam's own private tutor. Madam often took Alice along on her business trips, and while they traveled, Alice instructed Madam in penmanship, spelling and grammar, vocabulary, composition, public speaking, and etiquette as well as literature and current events. She was also one of the friends who exposed Madam to the arts and life's finer things. Ever since she was a young woman, Sarah Breedlove had thirsted for education and culture. Now, at age forty-four, she was finally filling in the gaps in her learning, thanks largely to Alice.

By 1913 Lelia had become restless in Pittsburgh. After several visits to New York City, she had fallen in love with its excitement and glamour. Harlem, in particular, was undergoing a blossoming of black culture that would come to be known as the Harlem Renaissance. Wanting to be in this exhilarating environment, Lelia suggested to her mother that the Madam Walker Company should have a location in New York City. Madam, always ready to expand, agreed. She bought a pair of adjacent townhouses in Harlem and had them remodeled into one building. Lelia, who by then was using Walker as her last name, would live on the top three floors, and on the ground floor would be the third—and most lavish—Lelia College of Beauty Culture, as well as a posh new salon. Lelia, of course, would manage the New York operation. Later that year, Madam bought her sister-in-law Lucy and her daughters a house in Los Angeles, where they would run a yet another new branch of the Walker Company.

Madam Walker was now forty-five years old. Only ten years earlier, she had been living in a small apartment, going bald, and washing clothes for a living, with Lelia struggling in school. Now Lelia's new salon was the finest beauty parlor in New York, even better than the ones for white women, and the Walker Company had operations from coast to coast. Madam Walker herself had been declared "America's foremost colored business woman" in the *Indianapolis Freeman*.

With Lelia in New York, Madam Walker continued traveling, going to the Caribbean and Central America to train agents to sell her products there, making the Walker Company an international corporation. Indianapolis remained her home base, however, and Madam planned to build a huge complex in that city. It would be a four-story building an entire block long, containing a large factory, offices, a beauty school, and a luxurious hair salon as well as restaurants, stores, and a ballroom for events.

One day, home in Indianapolis, Madam Walker went to the local theater to see a movie. The Isis Theater, like other establishments in those days, was segregated, and black customers were made to sit in the balcony. Madam knew this, but what she did not know was that the theater now charged black customers more for their tickets. When Madam handed the ticket girl a dime, the regular price of admission, the girl told her that the price for colored people had been raised to twenty-five cents. Furious, Madam left. She made up her mind then and there that her new Walker complex would include a movie theater for African Americans.

In 1916, after more traveling, Madam Walker decided to move to New York to be closer to Lelia. Indianapolis would remain her company headquarters, though, and she continued her plans to build the complex there. Leaving Alice Kelly in charge of the Indianapolis factory and F. B. Ransom in charge of the business there, Madam moved to the Harlem townhouse.

Living in Harlem, Madam bought some land in Irvington, New York, about twenty miles north of New York City on the Hudson River, and started building her dream home. Irvington's residents were mostly affluent white people, and Madam would be the only African American homeowner in the neighborhood. After the initial fuss died down, however, Madam would be accepted there with no trouble. After all, she was a well-known and wealthy entrepreneur. It would take a year to build the house, though. In the meantime, Madam resumed her travels.

While touring the South, Madam noticed that she was slowing down. She tired easily and felt a bit ill. She saw her doctor, who said that her blood pressure was very high and that she needed to rest for at least six weeks. Rest was something Madam hardly knew how to do, but her friends persuaded her to take a few weeks off and go to Hot Springs, Arkansas, where there was a famous resort with natural hot pools whose waters were believed to have healing properties. She stayed in Hot Springs for more than three months, from late November 1916 to mid-February 1917, with a long visit from Lelia in January. Madam left feeling much better.

Later that spring, in April 1917, the United States entered World War I, a conflict that had been raging in Europe for nearly three years. Madam Walker wanted to support the black soldiers, who served in segregated units. She traveled the country visiting the army's Negro training camps. Along with Lelia, she also joined the Circle for Negro War Relief, a group of African American women that raised funds for black soldiers. As part of the Circle, Lelia held a dance for black officers at her Harlem home to raise money to buy an ambulance for the black troops in France.

While the war was roaring overseas, terrible things were happening in the United States. More and more frequently, gangs of white men were lynching black people, meaning kidnapping and murdering them, often by hanging them from a tree or even tying them up and burning them alive. As these "lynching parties" terrorized African American communities, the local police usually did nothing about it. Sadly, racism, especially in the South, was acceptable to most white people in those days, and violence against black people was such an everyday occurrence that many whites paid little attention to it.

In July of 1917, after a race riot in East St. Louis, Illinois, left at least thirty-nine black people dead, Lelia and Madam Walker joined with African American leaders W.E.B. DuBois, James Weldon Johnson, and others to participate in a silent parade in New York, organized by the National Association for the Advancement of Colored People (NAACP, founded in 1901), to protest the lynchings and the riot killings. On that day, more than 5,000 people walked slowly down Fifth Avenue to a soft drumbeat, while 20,000 more watched quietly from the sidewalks. Later, in the fall of that year, Madam Walker toured the country to raise funds for the NAACP.

In August 1917 Madam held her first convention of Walker agents, whom she had organized into a union. Agents from across the country gathered in Philadelphia to exchange ideas and learn new techniques, with Madam giving demonstrations and motivational talks. Madam also announced the prizes that individual agents had won not only for making the most sales but also for raising the most money for charity. Madam believed in teaching Walker employees to always give back.

In June of 1918, shortly before the war ended, Madam Walker's thirty-four-room mansion was completed. As suggested by her friend Enrico Caruso, a famous Italian singer, she dubbed her new home Villa Lewaro—"villa" was the word for a grand Italian country home, and "Lewaro" came from Le-wa-ro, a shortened version of Lelia's name, Lelia Walker Robinson. Madam envisioned the estate as a "monument and inspiration" for black people. Although she planned to settle down there, spending her time gardening and entertaining prominent people, both black and white, she was not quite ready to do so yet.

In July, still involved with numerous charities and political organizations, Madam attended an event in Denver organized by the NACW (National Association of Colored Women). The gathering was held to celebrate the successful purchase of the Washington, D.C., home of illustrious civil-rights activist Frederick Douglass, who had died in 1895. The house would now be preserved as a historic site and museum. Madam herself donated $500 to the effort, making her the largest contributor, and at the event, she was invited to ceremonially burn the mortgage on the property.

After the war ended in November 1918, Madam Walker continued her charitable and political work, but she was beginning to feel ill again. She knew that her high blood pressure might have seriously damaged her kidneys, and she resolved to cut back on her traveling.

In April of 1919, though still feeling unwell, Madam decided to go to St. Louis to introduce some new Walker products as well as to visit her old friends at St. Paul's AME Church. While in St. Louis, she stayed with her good friend Jessie Robinson. But soon Madam became so sick that Jessie had a doctor and a nurse accompany her on a private train car back to New York City, and from there to Villa Lewaro.

Realizing she was going to die, Madam called F. B. Ransom to her bedside and gave him instructions on her last will. In mid-May, she slipped into a coma, and a few days later, on May 25, 1919, Sarah Breedlove Walker, age fifty-one, passed away. Her poignant last words, according to her doctor, were "I want to live to help my race." Of course, she had helped her race in myriad ways, but it is sad to think of how much more she wanted to do.

A thousand mourners, including Walker agents from all over the country, attended Madam Walker's funeral, held at Villa Lewaro. She was buried at Woodlawn Cemetery in the Bronx. Dozens of newspapers around the world carried Madam Walker's obituary. *New York Age* wrote, "The career of this self-made woman should be an incentive and an inspiration to all members of the race."

Madam Walker died a wealthy woman, with more than half a million dollars. In 1919, the year of her death, the Walker Company had 25,000 agents. Even after she died, the business continued to grow for several years, until the Great Depression came and the company verged on bankruptcy. Nevertheless, the Madam C. J. Walker Manufacturing Company stayed in business until the 1980s, when the rights to manufacture and sell Madam Walker's original formulas were sold to another company. Sales were slow and the Walker line languished until 2012, when a well-known cosmetics company called Sundial Brands took it over. Sundial plans to offer Madam Walker's products for sale again in 2016.

In her will, Madam Walker left thousands of dollars to various charities, schools, and civil-rights organizations. To Lelia she left one-third of the Walker Company, with the other two-thirds going into trust funds. She also left her estate, Villa Lewaro, to Lelia. Now privately owned and restored, Villa Lewaro was named a National Historic Landmark in 1976, and in 2012, the National Trust for Historic Preservation named the villa a National Treasure.

Shortly after Madam's funeral, Lelia got married, though she divorced her husband less than two years later. Around 1923 she changed her first name to A'Lelia. She remarried in 1926 but later divorced that husband too. In 1931, A'Lelia suffered a sudden stroke and died at age forty-six. In her will, she left the business to Mae and F. B. Ransom and left Villa Lewaro to the NAACP.

Mae was married in 1923, but she divorced her husband shortly after their first child, Walker Gordon Jackson, was born. In 1927 she married her second husband, Marion R. Perry, with whom she had a daughter, A'Lelia Mae Perry. Mae's granddaughter, A'Lelia Bundles, grew up to write two biographies of her great-great-grandmother, Madam C. J. Walker; one was a full-length book, *On Her Own Ground*, and the other was a shorter one for younger readers, *Madam C. J. Walker, Entrepreneur*. A'Lelia Bundles also maintains several websites.

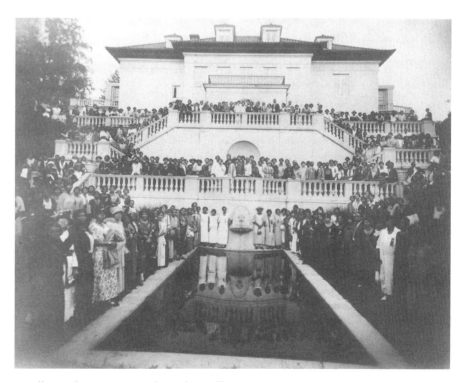

Walker sales agents gathered at Villa Lewaro in Irvington-on-Hudson, New York, 1924, several years after Madam Walker's death —Courtesy A'Lelia Bundles, Walker family collection

Although Madam Walker lived in Indianapolis only a few years, her legacy lives on in the Madam Walker Theatre Center, a major landmark in the city. After Madam's death, A'Lelia oversaw the construction of the block-long, four-story business complex her mother had been planning to build downtown. Completed in 1927, the new Madam C. J. Walker Manufacturing Company headquarters building housed a factory, offices, a beauty salon, a drugstore, a café, a ballroom, and, yes, a movie theater. The Walker Company used it until 1979, when it was purchased by a group of volunteers, who renovated it. In 1988 the restored building opened as the Madam C. J. Walker Urban Life Center. Now called the Madam Walker Theatre Center, the facility hosts regular theatrical and musical performances as well as cultural and educational programs. The center also contains a small museum dedicated to Madam Walker. The building was named a National Historic Landmark in 1991 and is listed on both the Indiana Register and the National Register of Historic Places.

Madam Walker herself has been honored in many ways. Numerous books, articles, videos, and websites have told her story. In 1987, filmmaker Stanley Nelson produced a documentary about Madam's life, called *Two Dollars and a Dream,* for national public television. In 1998, as part of the U.S. Postal Service's Black Heritage Commemorative Series, Madam Walker's image appeared on a postage stamp. She is also featured in the National Business Hall of Fame in Chicago's Museum of Science and Industry and in the National Women's Hall of Fame in Seneca Falls, New York. In 2013, a Charlotte, North Carolina, playwright named Kami Shalom wrote and performed a one-woman show based on Madam's life titled *Call Me Madam: The Making of an American Millionaire.*

Materials regarding Madam Walker can be found in the Indiana Historical Society's Walker Collection, as well as on A'Lelia Bundles's Madam Walker Family Archives website. Clearly, Madam C. J. Walker has not been forgotten.

Sarah Breedlove "Madam" Walker summed up her own inspiring philosophy in 1914 with these words:

> I am not merely satisfied in making money for myself, for I am endeavoring to provide employment for hundreds of women of my race. I had little or no opportunity when I started out in life. . . . I had to make my own living and my own opportunity. But I made it. That is why I want to say to every Negro woman present, don't sit down and wait for the opportunities to come. . . . Get up and make them!

Dorothy Buell (1886–1977) burning the midnight oil, 1950s
—Courtesy Calumet Regional Archives

10

DOROTHY BUELL

Dunes Preservationist

On Sunday, June 3, 1917, a crowd of 25,000 people gathered at Waverly Beach near the tiny town of Port Chester, Indiana, for an event called "The Dunes under Four Flags: An Historical Pageant of the Dunes of Indiana." It was a beautiful sunny day. Most of the visitors came by a special train, while others came by car, parking all over the roads around the beach. As they hiked over the sand dunes with their blankets and picnic baskets, the visitors came upon the breathtaking sight of slate-colored Lake Michigan shimmering beyond the golden dunes.

The people were there to watch five hundred actors and dancers play out the history of the dunes area. The performers were dressed as the people who lived or came through the dunes in the early days—Native American families; French, British, and American soldiers; fur traders, pioneers, and priests. As a whimsical touch, some even played woodland spirits. For four months, the players had been practicing their parts in the pageant. The event's organizers, a group called the National Dunes Park Association (NDPA), were trying to raise money for their effort to save the beautiful landscape known as the Indiana Dunes, hoping to turn the area into a national park.

In addition to vendor booths that sold refreshments and souvenirs was a first-aid station set up by the Red Cross to handle any health problems. Boy Scouts patrolled the hilltops, ready with semaphore flags to relay messages in case of an emergency. Campfire Girls wandered through the crowd selling life memberships in the NDPA for one dollar.

In the audience was thirty-year-old Dorothy Richardson (soon to become Dorothy Buell), who was there to watch her sister, Olive, perform with the dancers. Although she didn't know it yet, Dorothy would, later in life, devote the bulk of her time and energy to the cause of protecting the Indiana Dunes, bringing half a million people into her struggle against the most powerful industries and politicians in Indiana.

Years later, when someone asked her how she was able to fight so hard for so long, Dorothy would reply, with her renowned sense of humor, "I didn't know what I was getting into. When I found out, I didn't know how to stop."

Dorothy Richardson was born in Neenah, Wisconsin, in 1887. She was the youngest of Ambrose and Eliza Richardson's seven children, three girls and four boys. While Dorothy was growing up, the Richardson family spent their summers at a cottage in the Indiana Dunes, and Dorothy learned to cherish this unspoiled landscape. Yet even then, big corporations had their eye on the dunes for industrial development. A great struggle to preserve the dunes soon began, and many years later, as this struggle continued, Dorothy would find herself in the middle of it.

After finishing public elementary and high school in Neenah, Dorothy attended Milwaukee-Downer College before transferring to Lawrence College in Appleton, Wisconsin, from which she graduated in 1911 with a Bachelor of Arts degree in oratory (public speaking). After that, she took a job teaching speech and drama in Gary, Indiana.

In 1918, when she was thirty-one, Dorothy married James Harold "Hal" Buell. Hal was a mechanical engineer in Gary, but he moved frequently for his job. The Buells lived in Chicago as well as in Tulsa,

Oklahoma, and Flossmoor, Illinois. The couple's only child, Robert, was born in 1923. While Robert was growing up, Dorothy was a stay-at-home mom, although she was active in ladies' clubs. Whenever the Buells moved to a new place, Dorothy would organize a book club as a way of getting to know her new neighbors. A fan of theater and literature, she particularly enjoyed giving dramatic readings at club gatherings. She was also heavily involved in community theater.

When they lived in Illinois, the Buell family spent many summer weekends at Dorothy's childhood cottage in the Indiana Dunes. The cottage was in a lakeshore subdivision known as Ogden Dunes. A few miles away was an area called Waverly Beach. In 1925, thanks to the efforts of local preservationists, the three miles of lakefront at Waverly Beach became Indiana Dunes State Park.

In the late 1940s, with Robert grown and Hal retired, Hal and Dorothy moved to Ogden Dunes, where they built a larger home to replace the old vacation cottage. One day in 1949, as she and Hal were driving home from a vacation in White Sands National Monument in New Mexico, Dorothy started thinking about the dunes in her own backyard. People came from all over the world to see the White Sands, but Dorothy felt that its snow-colored dunes were not nearly as beautiful as the dunes in Indiana. "Her" dunes changed with the time of day—they could be lavender or deep purple in the evening, or turn from yellow to tan when the sun was bright. Some of them were "majestically bare," as she put it, while others wore "lacy shawls of vines."

That evening, Dorothy and Hal decided to have dinner at the Gary Hotel before driving the last few miles home. There, Dorothy saw a sign that said "Save the Dunes." Looking closer, she saw that there was to be a meeting of a group called the Indiana Dunes Preservation Council at the hotel that very evening. It was just what she had been thinking about! Turning to Hal, she said, "Let's go!"

With this meeting began the biggest political adventure of Dorothy Buell's life.

The group that had called that meeting, the Indiana Dunes Preservation Council (IDPC), was composed of several organizations that had joined together for a common cause—to protect the dunes from development. Among the concerned groups were the National Dunes Park Association (which had been fighting to save the duneland for more than forty years), the Boy Scouts, the Audubon Society, and the American Legion. Leading the meeting was Dr. Reuben Strong, a University of Chicago professor and ornithologist from the Chicago Conservation Council. Dr. Strong was an important person whom Dorothy would get to know.

The meeting was called to discuss a new threat to the dunes that had recently emerged: several steel companies and other interested parties were lobbying Congress to build a port in the dunes area, at Burns Ditch on the Lake Michigan shore, for industrial development. The proposed site encompassed three miles of natural lakeshore, in the spot where the best dunes were located. If a port was built, the shore and dunes there would be destroyed. Yet, besides the companies who would be building there, many Indiana politicians, groups, and citizens supported the port proposal because it would create jobs and grow the local economy. The IDPC argued that preserving the area for visitors would also be good for the economy, since tourism was a growing industry in it own right.

Interestingly, three older steel companies that were already based in the area—Inland Steel, Youngstown Steel, and U.S. Steel—were also against the port, but for a different reason: it would bring them new competition. Because of this, representatives from the three companies also attended the meeting that evening.

The issues discussed at the IDPC meeting captured Dorothy's interest and also her heart. She attended subsequent meetings of the IDPC and of Reuben Strong's group, the Chicago Conservation Council, becoming increasingly passionate about saving the dunes. At a Chicago Conservation Council meeting in early 1952, Dr. Strong noted that both the IDPC and the old NDPA had fallen apart, and there was no one left to take up the fight against overdevelopment in the dunes. Did anyone have any ideas about who might be able to reignite the movement?

Dorothy spoke up. She reminded the group of the efforts of the NDPA of the 1910s and '20s, which had successfully lobbied for the creation of the Indiana Dunes State Park in 1925, protecting more than 2,000 acres of duneland. One of the major leaders in that effort, she noted, was Bess Sheehan.

Born Bess May Vrooman in 1882, Bess Sheehan was one of the organizers of the "Dunes under Four Flags" pageant that Dorothy had attended in 1917. As the leader of the Dunes Park Committee of the Indiana Federation of Women's Clubs and an officer of the National Dunes Park Association, Bess had used her connections with area women's clubs and nature groups to push through the establishment of the state park, proving that a group of dedicated women could garner the necessary resources, including their own passion and energy, to stand up to powerful opposition.

Recalling Bess's example, Dorthy suggested that perhaps women could lead a new movement to save the dunes.

Listening to Dorothy's words, Dr. Strong admired the enthusiasm she showed. A few days later, he wrote to her, asking if she herself might lead the new dunes movement. She hesitated. She had never been a leader on a project this big. She replied that she would have to think it over. Sixty-five years old at that time, she was only a few years younger than Bess Sheehan. But her health was good and her commitment to the cause was unwavering.

Finally, after months of pondering, Dorothy made up her mind to take up the cause as its leader. Her first step was to recruit helpers, starting with the women who lived in the dunes region. She would hold a meeting in her home and invite all the women she knew who might be interested, including Bess Sheehan. Now seventy, Bess still lived in the area, though she was currently involved in other causes. But Dorothy knew that with her experience, Bess would be a big help in launching a new save-the-dunes campaign.

Dorothy put on her hat and white gloves, as she always did when she went out, and visited each of her women neighbors in Ogden Dunes, Bess Sheehan among them, asking them to attend the meeting at her home. On June 20, 1952, Bess and twenty other women gathered at Dorothy's house. Bess opened the meeting by recounting the history of preservation efforts in the dunes and her own experiences with the NDPA. She told the group how she not only persuaded large companies and local businesses to make big donations but also collected pennies from schoolchildren to help the cause. She described how she and groups of her supporters went to talk to state lawmakers and their wives, sometimes stopping legislators in the hallways to ask them to vote on the dunes park bill.

Bess warned the ladies, however, that their chances of succeeding were slim. Stopping the port would be virtually impossible. Several local newspapers were controlled by the steel industry and other companies that wanted the port built, so much of the general public supported it too.

The women at the meeting decided not to try to stop the port but rather to focus on expanding the established state park's boundaries, adding five miles of lakeshore. Calling themselves the Save the Dunes Council, the ladies announced their intentions to the press. The group's goal, Dorothy said, was the "preservation of the Indiana Dunes for public use and enjoyment," and she declared that "We are prepared to spend the rest of our lives if necessary to save the dunes."

As the council well knew, many forces opposed its mission. Four huge corporations had plans to build in the area the council was trying to protect. Much of the land was owned by a Texas multimillionaire who wanted to sell the sand. Furthermore, with the St. Lawrence Seaway scheduled to open in 1959, oceangoing ships would soon be sailing over the Great Lakes, bringing jobs and dollars to port towns along the lakeshore. Local newspapers, Indiana governor Harold Handley, and the chambers of commerce in Porter County all wanted the prosperity they thought a port would bring. Building it would require federal funding, but port supporters had a number of U.S. congressmen in their corner, including Senator

Homer Capehart and Representative Charles Halleck. Opposing such a coalition would be a tough battle.

After putting her initial reservations aside, Dorothy Buell was an excellent leader. A petite lady and very proper, she addressed everyone by their last name. Yet despite her formality, she had a special way with people. When Dorothy got up to speak, you could hear a pin drop. According to one Save the Dunes Council member, she could "silence a roomful of enemies with a meaningful incline of her white curly head."

One of Dorothy's secrets was never to say anything negative about those who disagreed with her, but simply to share her views on the importance of saving the beauty of nature. She was far from timid about facing up to people, however. Whenever she asked someone to join the cause, she would not listen to the person's reasons for saying no—she just kept asking until the person finally said yes.

Following Dorothy's lead, the Save the Dunes Council vowed not to say anything bad about steel mills or about the people who opposed their efforts. Instead, the women focused on educating the public about the majesty of the dunes. The council used every method its members could think of to get the word out. They printed pamphlets with gorgeous photos of the dunes. They organized nature walks and sponsored events such as art and photo contests to encourage people to visit the dunes. They published articles, wrote letters, held meetings, led protests, and gave talks.

Another priority for the council was raising money, not only to help spread the word but also to buy as much duneland as they could before the corporations got to it. They encouraged conservation-minded people everywhere to join the council, setting their dues at only one dollar. They talked to the members of their women's clubs, locally and nationwide, about supporting the Save the Dunes Council. They sent newsletters to members, keeping them informed about progress or setbacks in their campaign and asking for donations.

Council members used their personal skills and talents to advance the cause. Artists and photographers published pictures of the dunes, and writers wrote articles about them. Scientists did studies of the ecology of the dunes, reporting their findings in science journals. Lawyers followed the progress of laws that affected the dunes, while engineers and architects studied the various plans for construction and industrial development in the area, exposing any mistakes or inaccuracies they found.

As support for saving the dunes grew, the council turned its attention to lawmakers. Dorothy and other council members testified many times in front of legislative committees on the state and national levels. Herb Read, one of the first male members of the Save the Dunes Council, said about Dorothy, "When she testified at a hearing, the members were compelled by her presence to treat her with respect even when they hated the point of view she stood for." Over the course of the movement, Herb Read, Reuben Strong, and many other men would help the cause, but it was the women who got things started and supplied much of the labor through the years.

After only one year, the Save the Dunes Council had two thousand members, comprising people from every state. It was in this first year that the council had its first success. Members learned that an important parcel in the dunes was up for sale. The property encompassed a marshy area called Cowles Bog, where scientist Henry Cowles had made important discoveries about dunes ecology. The farmer who owned the fifty-six acres around Cowles Bog could not pay his taxes, so the land was to be auctioned, and it might go for a very low price.

The Save the Dunes Council had $125 in its own treasury, plus $751 from Bess Sheehan, who had given the council the money left over from the treasury of the old National Dunes Park Association. The group had also received a gift of $700 from Mrs. Norton Barker in Michigan City. The council members didn't know what the final price would be, but they hoped they would have enough. Hal Buell went to the sale with his checkbook, ready to put in any additional money needed, which in the end amounted to $153. He wrote the check, and Cowles Bog became the property of the Save the Dunes Council. This land was the beginning of what would eventually become the Indiana Dunes National Lakeshore.

In 1954 the council formed a board of directors that included prominent scientists, artists, writers, conservationists, and wealthy philanthropists. By 1956 the group was on its way to raising a million dollars, and members had started a petition that within two years would have a half a million signatures. By then the council had gained the support of national conservation groups and of National Parks director Conrad Wirth.

At the same time, however, two major companies, Midwest Steel and Bethlehem Steel, were speeding up their efforts to buy land and build factories in the dunes, and they amped up their pressure on the federal government to build a port for them. Meanwhile, their allies in the media continued to influence public opinion in the port's favor. Dorothy was getting discouraged—the council needed more support, and fast. Someone suggested that Dorothy contact Sen. Paul Douglas of Illinois, thinking he might be interested in helping, since he had a small weekend house in the dunes.

When Dorothy first wrote to Senator Douglas about helping, he turned her down, saying he did not think he should get involved in another state's disagreements. But as usual, Dorothy would not take no for an answer. Knowing that nature writer Donald Peattie and his wife were longtime friends of the senator and Mrs. Douglas, Dorothy wrote to Peattie in California, asking him to help her persuade Senator Douglas to join the movement. Mrs. Peattie replied that her husband was in ill health and could not do it.

Rather than give up, Dorothy tried harder. She traveled to California, where her son, Robert, and his family lived, to enjoy a visit with them but also for another purpose. While there, she went to the Peatties' home. The maid would not let her in, saying that Mr. Peattie was near death, but Dorothy insisted on speaking with Mrs. Peattie. When the lady of the house came to the door, Dorothy turned on her famous dignified charm. Finally won over,

Mrs. Peattie promised to write to Mrs. Douglas and urge her to ask the senator to support the Save the Dunes Council.

Dorothy's plan worked. Senator Douglas finally agreed to help the council with its mission. In fact, he soon embraced the cause wholeheartedly—after all, he loved the Indiana duneland himself. As an advocate for the labor unions in Illinois, Douglas also won union support for the council. In Congress, he introduced various bills in support of preserving the dunes. In the end, Paul Douglas's involvement was instrumental in curbing development in the region and in getting the dunes made into a national park.

Over the next several years, thanks to the efforts of the Save the Dunes Council, people all over the country came to know about the situation in the Indiana Dunes, and more and more of them began to favor the creation of a duneland national park. Yet Congress paid no attention. Senator Douglas had submitted bill after bill proposing

Dorothy Buell leads visitors from the National Park Service through the dunes, 1970s. —Courtesy Calumet Regional Archives

a park, but each was rejected in turn. Nevertheless, he stood firm. In 1960, when a report came out concluding that Burns Ditch would be an ideal place to build a port, Douglas persuaded his fellow legislators to hold off on approving its construction. Why were no other sites evaluated? he asked. And why were the concerns about this site being ignored? By this time, the public clearly wanted a national park, so why was Congress not looking into that possiblity?

In 1961 Douglas approached the newly elected president, John F. Kennedy, about the dunes problem. After weighing both sides of the argument, Kennedy decided on a compromise. The port would be built, but the government would also establish a 14,000-acre national park along the dunes lakeshore. The council had known from the start that the port was inevitable, so they were quite happy to have succeeded in protecting an important section of the duneland.

The Indiana Dunes National Lakeshore opened in 1966. Afterward, Senator Douglas sent Dorothy a telegram saying "We have at last achieved our victory. Your leadership and your ability to keep together the best conservation group in the country made this possible." At the park's official dedication ceremony, which was not held until 1972, Dorothy Buell was an honored guest. Sadly, Bess Sheehan was not there—she had died in 1968.

In 1970 Dorothy and Hal Buell moved to Palo Alto, California, to be near their son and their three grandchildren. Hal died soon after the move. Dorothy died in a San Jose nursing home in 1977. She was ninety years old. Her remains were taken back to her hometown of Neenah, Wisconsin, for burial.

Even after the Indiana Dunes National Lakeshore was established, the Save the Dunes Council was still not finished with its work—the group remained active in seeking more land for the park. Thanks to the council's continued efforts, Congress approved additional park acreage in 1976, 1980, 1986, and 1992. In 1993, the visitor center at Indiana Dunes National Lakeshore was officially dedicated as the Dorothy Buell Memorial Visitor Center.

The Save the Dunes Council, Dorothy Buell's legacy, still exists today, overseeing park improvements, giving advice to other environmental groups, and keeping an ever-watchful eye on the precious, fragile land of the Indiana Dunes.

As park superintendent Dale Engquist once said, "These dunes have not been saved by the Park Service or by Congress. They have been saved by the people who love them." Among the people who loved them the most was Dorothy Richardson Buell.

Vivian Carter (1921–1989), circa 1953 —Courtesy Calumet Regional Archives

11

VIVIAN CARTER

Radio Deejay and Record Producer

"Good evening. You're listening to *Livin' with Vivian* on WWCA, Gary. I'm Vivian Carter, the hostess who brings you the mostest."

The rich, booming voice was familiar to the radio listeners of northwestern Indiana in the 1950s. Six nights a week, on her five-hour show, deejay Vivian Carter played a mixture of blues, gospel, jazz, and "doo-wop," a catchy form of rhythm and blues (R&B). At the time, these music genres were commonly called "race music," meaning music performed by African Americans. In the early days, Vivian played mostly black music for black listeners, but soon race music, especially R&B, caught on among white teenagers as well. Before long, rhythm and blues, combined with elements of "white" country and western and other styles, evolved into a genre called rock and roll. Vivian embraced these exciting new sounds, recognizing what her growing listenership wanted to hear.

It was 1953, a very busy year for Vivian Carter. In addition to her radio show, she and her soon-to-be husband, James (Jimmy) Bracken, owned a popular record store in Gary called Vivian's Record Shop. Now she and Jimmy were launching a new business—a record company called Vee-Jay Records (Vee for Vivian, Jay for Jimmy). In time, the company would become legendary for its meteoric rise and spectacular fall.

Vivian Precious Carter was born on March 25, 1921, in Tunica, Mississippi, to Ludie and Minnie Carter. When Vivian was three, the Carter family, including Ludie's parents, Tony and Rosie Carter, moved to Gary, Indiana. Vivian's only sibling, her brother, Calvin, was born in Gary in 1925. Their father worked as a laborer in a dairy, and later in a steel mill. When the children were teenagers, Minnie opened a restaurant in Gary's Midtown neighborhood.

As in most cities in those days, Gary's schools were segregated. Vivian and Calvin attended the local public schools for "colored" children. In sixth grade, Vivian won first place in a public-speaking contest as well as first place in a citywide track meet. In 1934 she entered Roosevelt High School, considered an excellent secondary school for African American students. After school, Vivian worked as a waitress at her mother's restaurant.

YJean Chambers, Vivian's friend at Roosevelt High, described Vivian as lively, extroverted, and full of fun, with a low-pitched, full voice that seemed to have its own built-in microphone. Although Vivian was just average in most classes, she was outstanding in public speaking and dramatics. She was active in all school plays, was elected president of the student council, and was the head cheerleader for the school's sports teams. When Vivian discovered that girls were not allowed to be in the school's concert band, she went to the principal and persuaded him to change that unfair rule.

After graduating from high school in 1939, Vivian moved to Chicago, taking classes at Cortez-Peters Business College. To support herself, she waited tables at the Cotton Club, a well-known African American nightclub on Chicago's Near South Side.

In December 1941, the United States entered World War II. Soon afterward, Vivian took a job as a clerk for the Quartermaster General's Office (army supply depot) in Washington, D.C. After about six months, she asked to be transferred to the Chicago office. Later she transferred to the Signal Corps (radio and radar communications) in Chicago. Vivian was in the Signal Corps when she met her future husband and business partner, Jimmy Bracken, a music lover from Kansas City, in 1944. At the time, Jimmy was thirty-five and Vivian was twenty-three.

After the war, Vivian returned to waitressing, working at a South Side night spot called Club DeLisa. One day in 1948, she was listening to the radio, tuned to the black station WGES, when deejay Al Benson announced that he was looking for two young deejays, a guy and a girl, for a new segment. He was holding a contest, he said, to see who could write and read the best one-minute radio commercial. The winners would be given their own fifteen-minute radio shows. Benson told his listeners that the auditions would be held that evening at seven o'clock at a downtown hotel.

As Vivian recalled, "[It] was like ten minutes to six when I heard about it. I hadn't even thought about a commercial, but I listened to his commercial on a clothing store and jotted down notes while he was talking. And I wrote my commercial that way."

When she arrived at the hotel, she said, "There must have been eight hundred or a thousand people there to get an audition." Upon meeting Vivian, Benson must have recognized some inborn talent in her because she won the contest, making her the first black female disc jockey in Chicago. The male winner was Sid McCoy, who later joined Vivian and Jimmy's record company. In the 1970s, McCoy became the announcer for *Soul Train*, a long-running TV show that featured the music of black performers.

After working at WGES for a few months, Vivian moved back to Gary, working as an assistant on deejay Eddie Honesty's *Rockin' and Rhythm Show* at WJOB in nearby Hammond, Indiana. Vivian stayed at this job for several years, learning about the radio business.

In 1950, while she was still at WJOB, Vivian and her longtime boyfriend, Jimmy Bracken, opened a record store in Gary, Vivian's Record Shop. Because people knew her name from the radio show, the store thrived. Jerry Locasto, who was a teenager in Hammond in the 1950s, remembered driving with friends after school to Vivian's Record Shop. Groups of both black and white teenagers, he said, would gather to watch through the window as the outgoing Vivian spun record after record of great new sounds. She played their requests and talked to them about what music they liked and didn't like. Knowing what young people wanted to hear gave Vivian an advantage over the competition.

In 1952 Vivian landed a deejay job at WGRY in Gary, where she hosted two morning programs, *The Vivian Carter Show*, which played popular music, and *Vivian's Spiritual Hour*, which was devoted to gospel music and religious discussion. Finally, in 1953, Vivian got her own late-night program, *Livin' with Vivian*, at the larger Gary station, WWCA.

Henry Farag, an eleven-year-old Gary resident in 1956, remembers the moment he first heard Vivian Carter's "booming, . . . rapid-fire, throaty voice," which he said "almost blew my skull apart." Young Henry had received a kit for building a crystal radio, and when he put it together and got it working, he heard Vivian's voice, "aggressive and bombastic, but cheerful as she touted a record, sometimes playing it three or four times in a row." The music was something Henry had never heard before—a smooth but spicy sound called rhythm and blues. "The experience, to a prepubescent white boy, was slightly scary but exhilarating," Farag recalled. He instantly became a fan of *Livin' with Vivian*, and R&B became his passion. Henry Farag grew up to work in the music industry himself, and he became a close friend of his childhood idol, Vivian Carter.

The music Vivian played on her show was "race music," such as blues, gospel, black jazz, and R&B. Much of this music was not readily available on records. Some of what Vivian played on the radio were old 78 rpm discs, a type of record that by the 1950s had largely been replaced by 45 rpm singles. She may also have played private recordings of live performances, unavailable commercially. Other records were simply rare and hard to find because few copies had been produced. Mainstream (that is, white) record stores seldom carried much, if any, black music, and black record stores were few. Moreover, many fine black musicians had never been recorded at all. As the popularity of race music grew, the demand was becoming greater than the supply, and Vivian recognized an opportunity.

Vivian and Jimmy began saving their money to start a business recording black artists and selling the records. The fact that Vivian could play these records on the radio and promote them in her store would give their company some built-in marketing. But where to begin? As it happened, she found the answer "in her own backyard."

After winning a talent competition at Roosevelt High School (Vivian's own alma mater), a group of five students calling themselves the Spaniels were invited to play at the school's graduation dinner in June 1953. Vivian was there. The five boys had been playing together, often on street corners, for some time, and they had recently changed their band's name to the Spaniels because one of their girlfriends said they sounded like a bunch of dogs. Apparently Vivian felt that they sounded much better than dogs because, according to the Spaniels' Willie Jackson, she "took notice of our performance and decided then and there . . . to place the group under contract."

Vivian started rehearsing with the young group in her mother's garage. When she and Jimmmy felt the Spaniels were ready to make a record, they borrowed $500 from a local pawnbroker and paid for a session of studio time at Universal Studios in Chicago. Here the group recorded their first single, a song called "Baby, It's You," written by band members James "Pookie" Hudson and Gerald Gregory. Vivian and Jimmy had no means of distribution yet, so they took the record to Chance Records company and made a deal with them to release it.

"Baby, It's You" was a hit, reaching number ten on the R&B chart. With this initial success, Vee-Jay Records was born. Soon after this, perhaps flushed with the promise of their new venture, Vivian and Jimmy got married on December 16, 1953, in a spur-of-the-moment ceremony at the offices of United Record Distributors in Chicago.

Vee-Jay recorded about twelve other singles that first year, including a song called "High and Lonesome" by Chicago blues singer Jimmy Reed. The record was a moderate seller, but Reed's next single, "You Don't Have to Go," released in 1954, was a chart-topper. The future was looking bright for Vivian and Jimmy.

Shortly after Vee-Jay was organized, Vivian's brother, Calvin Carter, who had some experience in the music industry, joined the company as a producer and the director of what is called the Artists and Repertoire (A&R) department. A&R people are the ones who choose the performers and approve the songs. Calvin also helped the artists compose original songs. Pookie Hudson said he didn't start writing songs because he wanted to write songs but because Vivian and Jimmy insisted on original material. This turned out to be a good thing—Hudson's songs were, more often than not, big hits.

The Spaniels' next recording for Vee-Jay was another Hudson composition, "Goodnite, Sweetheart, Goodnite," released in the spring of 1954. This record was an even bigger hit than the first one, landing at number five on the R&B charts. As the song's popularity grew, it became a "crossover" hit, meaning a black record that crossed over racial lines to become a hit with white listeners. Later the same year, a white group, the McGuire Sisters, recorded Hudson's song, and their version became a million seller. Like many songs in those days, "Goodnite, Sweetheart, Goodnite" was essentially stolen by competitors—Hudson received no royalties for other artists' recordings of his composition until the 1990s.

The fact that another record company was making money on their song did not necessarily bother Vivian and Jimmy. The Spaniels' original version was a hit in its own right, and it proved that African American music could have broad appeal. But Vivian took a lesson from the experience. Knowing that music that sounded "white" sold better than music that sounded "black," she told Calvin to add more mainstream elements to the arrangements on Vee-Jay's records, hoping to widen their audience.

After Vee-Jay's early success with the Spaniels and Jimmy Reed, Vivian and Jimmy moved the company from Gary to Chicago in 1954. By that time, Vee-Jay had its own system for distributing records, so Vivian and Jimmy no longer had to pay Chance Records to put their discs out. As it happened, Chance Records went out of business at the end of 1954. Soon afterward, Vivian and Jimmy hired one of the company's accountants, Ewart Abner, to manage

Vee-Jay's business office. Although Vivian, Jimmy, and Calvin had excellent ears for what music the public would like, they did not know so much about handling money and paperwork. For this they would rely on Abner.

Now established in Chicago, Vee-Jay produced more hit records, including "For Your Precious Love" by Jerry Butler and the Impressions, which sold a million copies in 1958. The company continued to produce black music such as gospel, blues, jazz, doo-wop, and the newly emerging "soul" genre. Some of these records crossed over to the "Hot 100" pop charts. Before long, Vee-Jay's success began to attract some of Chicago's top performers, such as blues singer John Lee Hooker, doo-wop groups the Dells and the El Dorados, gospel group the Staple Singers, and jazzman Buddy de Franco. Rhythm and blues remained a Vee-Jay mainstay. Among the label's top sellers were "Duke of Earl" by Gene Chandler and Dee Clark's "Raindrops," both released in 1961. Vee-Jay also recorded a group called the Pips, who later made it big as Gladys Knight and the Pips.

With the successes of 1961, Vivian and Jimmy promoted Ewart Abner to president of Vee-Jay Records. Jimmy and Vivian still made the final decisions, but when it came to making deals, Abner was the boss. He knew more about business and had insight into what was happening. Unfortunately, he also had a gambling problem. Vivian and Jimmy would later discover that Abner took company money and lost it gambling.

In 1962, Vee-Jay signed its first white artists, a pop-rock group called the Four Seasons. The band's first single, "Sherry," rocketed to number one. The next two Four Seasons singles also hit number one. Vee-Jay was on top of the world.

Vivian enjoyed her newfound wealth and status. She was always dressed to the nines and rode around in a gold Cadillac. She and Jimmy threw lavish parties. Vivian liked to spread the money around, too; some said she was generous to a fault.

With the Four Seasons' extraordinary success, Vee-Jay began looking for more white artists. By that time, word was coming across the Atlantic about a popular Australian-British crooner named Frank Ifield, who had produced three number-one hits in a row in England. Vee-Jay wanted to see if they could reproduce that success in America. They approached Ifield's British label, EMI, which was having a little trouble breaking into the American market. EMI was particularly eager to try out on Americans a new English rock group called the Beatles, who were becoming enormously popular in Great Britain but were virtually unknown in the States. The label had already tried to get its American counterpart, Capitol Records, to release a single by the Beatles, but Capitol was not interested. When Vee-Jay came along asking about Frank Ifield, EMI proposed that Vee-Jay take the Beatles, too, as a package deal. The Beatles' sound was not the kind that Vee-Jay normally handled, but in order to get Frank Ifield, they agreed to distribute the Beatles records.

Vee-Jay immediately released Ifield's "I Remember You," which landed at number five on the Hot 100. Not bad. The Beatles' "Please Please Me," released in the spring of 1963, did not fare as well, though. The single, along with two other singles and an unreleased LP album called *Introducing the Beatles*, sat on the back shelf for about a year.

By that time, in spite of producing hit after hit, Vee-Jay was having money problems. Vivian and Jimmy had become victims of their own success, as the demand for their records was so great that the label could no longer keep up with production. To make matters worse, company president Ewart Abner had been keeping poor financial records, and the Four Seasons, as well as other artists, began complaining that they were not being paid their royalties. In 1963, both Four Seasons and Frank Ifield canceled their contracts with Vee-Jay. By then it was also becoming apparent that Abner was gambling with the company's funds. In addition, the government was looking into Vee-Jay's failure to pay sufficient income taxes. Vivian and Jimmy fired Abner in August 1963, hoping to turn things around.

In the meantime, the Beatles' aggressive manager, Brian Epstein, who was convinced that Americans would love the charming foursome and their upbeat music, arranged for the group to perform on the immensely popular American television variety program *The Ed Sullivan Show*. Within weeks of the Beatles' appearance on Sullivan's show in February of 1964, "Beatlemania" had taken hold of the USA. Vee-Jay immediately re-released "Please Please Me" along with "From Me to You" and "Do You Want to Know a Secret?" as well as the Beatles' LP album.

By 1964, with the Beatles and its other hit-making artists, Vee-Jay was taking in millions of dollars a year. No doubt assuming that the company's financial problems would be worked out, Vivian and Jimmy moved their headquarters to Los Angeles and bought a mansion in Beverly Hills. Vivian's brother, Calvin Carter, who remained in the Chicago office, recalled that the company "went from fifteen or twenty employees to about two hundred overnight. The growth was just too fast."

Not surprisingly, Capitol Records, which had earlier passed up the opportunity to distribute the Beatles' music in America, now wanted another chance at them. Capitol had already picked up a few new Beatles' singles from EMI, but they now wanted exclusive American rights to the group's recordings. Over the next couple of years, Capitol filed a number of lawsuits against Vee-Jay, costing the company a fortune in legal fees. At the same time, Vee-Jay was tied up with other lawsuits, from the Four Seasons' manager and others, for royalty payments. Last but not least, the U.S. Internal Revenue Service (IRS) was investigating the label's financial affairs.

By court order, Vee-Jay lost its rights to sell Beatles records in October 1964. As word got around in the record industry that Vee-Jay was having money troubles, other artists left the label as well. In 1965 Vivian and Jimmy moved their headquarters back to Chicago and tried to keep the company going, but it was too little, too late. Vivian and Jimmy could not pay Vee-Jay's back taxes, and the IRS took everything they had, even their record store in Gary. In 1966 Vee-Jay declared bankruptcy. Even faster than it had risen to the top of the music industry, Vee-Jay Records went out of business.

In spite of Vee-Jay's ultimate demise, it is unfair to call it a failure. The label carved out a place of honor not only in African American music history, but in all of modern music history. In addition to the wonderful songs that Vivian and her partners produced, Vee-Jay paved the way for other black record labels, including Detroit's legendary Motown Records. Gary businessman Gordon Keith, a close friend of Vivian, called her "the mother of the black recording industry."

With Vee-Jay closed, Vivian returned to Gary and to radio, hosting a late-night gospel show on WWCA. It's unclear whether she and Jimmy separated at some point, but Jimmy, presumably without Vivian, tried and failed to launch a new record company; later he opened a record store, again without his wife. At the time of Jimmy's death from lung cancer in Chicago in 1972, Vivian was working at WGRT, Chicago. Vivian and Jimmy never had children. Four years later, while still doing her radio show, Vivian took a day job with Calumet Township Trustee Office in Gary, where she worked until her health began to decline in 1982.

After Vee-Jay's demise, Calvin Carter, who was married and had two sons, continued producing music for other companies. He was living in Gary when he died in 1986.

In Vivian's later years, her high school friend YJean Chambers visited her often. YJean said that Vivian was philosophical about her "rags to riches to rags" life story. "I don't miss a thing now," Vivian told her. "That's all behind me." YJean observed that "in reflection, she felt that success having come so easily, and being unused to great wealth, she did not know the trick of looking over the shoulders of those who work for you and watching the accounts and the books."

Vivian spent her final days in hospitals and nursing homes. Due to her untreated diabetes, she suffered amputations of her feet, one hand, and several fingers. Later, her high blood pressure led to a stroke. Shortly before she died, her first star, James "Pookie" Hudson of the Spaniels, visited her in the nursing home and sang by her bedside the group's first big hit, "Goodnite, Sweetheart, Goodnite."

Vivian Carter died on June 12, 1989, at age sixty-eight. She is far from forgotten, however. In 1995 Indiana University Northwest presented a daylong tribute to Vivian and Vee-Jay Records, with speakers and performances. Vee-Jay was also one of the topics of a 2006 exhibit, "100 plus One: Celebrating America's Music Before Motown and Beyond," at the DuSable Museum of African American History. In 2012 the Chicago Dramatists Theatre hosted a staged reading of a musical called *Vee-Jay Records: The Little Record Company That Almost. . . .* Two years later, Vivian's friend Henry Farag wrote, directed, and produced a musical about Vee-Jay called *The Signal: A Doo-Wop Rhapsody*. There has also been talk of a feature film about Vivian's life, tentatively titled *Vivian*. Since 2010, a growing effort has been made to nominate Vivian Carter, as well as the Spaniels, for induction into the Rock and Roll Hall of Fame.

As for Vee-Jay's music, much has been re-released since Vivian's death. Over the years, several different owners have controlled the company's catalog of recordings. Rockwood Music Group put out a box set of Vee-Jay R&B songs in 1993, and in 2007, Shout! Factory produced a box set called *Vee-Jay: The Definitive Collection*. Although Vee-Jay, Vivian, Jimmy, and Calvin are gone, the music will live on.

In a time when black and white teens were mostly kept separated, the music played at Vivian's Record Shop in Gary, Indiana, brought them together. In the record business, this was called "crossover" music, but to Vivian Carter, it was just wonderful music that was too good not to share.

Margaret Ray (1921–2008) in her dress uniform, circa 1944
—Courtesy Marsha Wright

MARGARET RAY RINGENBERG

Passionate Pilot

"Margaret Jane, there's a telegram for you!" exclaimed Luella Scheuman, slightly out of breath. Luella was the Ray family's neighbor in Hoagland, Indiana.

Why on earth would I be getting a telegram? thought Margaret, who had earned her private pilot's license only a few months earlier. It was February 1943. The United States was at war. But the Rays had no family members in the service, so the telegram could not have been one of those thousands sent by the army to notify loved ones of a combat death.

Margaret Jane was to call Western Union, Luella said, to receive the message. The Rays had no telephone in their house, so when they needed to make a call, they just used the Scheumans' phone.

Next door, Margaret Jane wrote down the message as the operator read it to her: IF INTERESTED IN WOMEN FLYING TRAINING FOR FERRY COMMAND CONTACT ME PALMER HOUSE CHICAGO TUESDAY THRU THURSDAY FEBRUARY 16TH 17TH 18TH FOR INTERVIEW. It was signed Ethel Sheehy, Chief Recruiting Officer. Margaret had no idea what a "ferry command" was or why the army was recruiting women. But as she soon discovered, three other young women she knew from flight school had received the same telegram.

A few days later, breathless with excitement, the four young pilots boarded a train bound for Chicago.

Margaret Jane Ray was born in Fort Wayne on June 17, 1921, the youngest of Albert and Lottie Ray's three daughters. When Margaret Jane (the family called her by her full name) was seven, the Rays moved from Fort Wayne to a farm in Hoagland, about fifteen miles southeast of the city. Her sister Mary was nine years older than she, and Violet was seven years older, so Margaret Jane often played by herself. She didn't mind—she liked having her freedom and independence.

Margaret Jane loved the farm. She had a horse to ride, fields to run and play in, and animals to care for. Her dad even taught her to drive his big tractor. Whatever she did, she dug in with all her energy, of which she had an abundance. Margaret Jane knew she was lucky. It was the middle of the Great Depression, but her family always had plenty to eat from the farm, and her father had a regular income from his job at General Electric (he hired men to do most of the heavy farm work).

One Sunday afternoon, the Ray family was taking a drive when they spotted a plane coming in for a landing in a cornfield. As the family stopped to watch, the pilot jumped out and walked across the field to their car. "Want to go for a ride?" he asked.

Margaret Jane's father, Albert, wrinkled his brow. "How much?" he inquired.

The next thing she knew, Margaret Jane was climbing into the little plane with her dad and her two sisters. At the last minute, her mother got into the plane too, saying that if they were all going to die, she might as well die with them.

The flight was exciting, and of course the plane landed safely. Eight-year-old Margaret Jane had no idea at the time that flying planes would become the focus of her life.

Eight years later, at age sixteen, Margaret Jane took her second plane ride. She and a friend were hanging around Smith Field in Fort

Wayne—Margaret Jane loved to watch the planes coming in and going out—when a young pilot approached the girls and offered to take them up for free. They eagerly accepted.

Somehow that trip was even more thrilling than the first one had been. Back on the ground, Margaret Jane began to wonder how she might fly all the time—she would love going to new places and seeing new sights every day. By the time she graduated from Hoagland High School, Margaret Jane Ray had made up her mind. She would study to become a flight attendant (or, as they were called then, a stewardess). The thought of being a pilot never even crossed her mind—commercial airlines hired only male pilots, and only men flew in wartime. Other than Amelia Earhart, Margaret knew of no female pilots.

To become a stewardess, Margaret Jane learned, she would need a nursing degree, which was a requirement for the job in those days. In order to earn money for nursing school, Margaret Jane, with her father's help, got a job at the General Electric plant where he worked. Now she and her dad rode to and from work together every day.

As she contemplated her future, Margaret Jane began to worry about what would happen if, when she was a stewardess, the pilot got sick or had a heart attack. She thought it would be good idea to learn a little about flying, at least enough to land an airplane in an emergency. So one morning, riding to work with her father, Margaret Jane said, "I want to learn to fly an airplane." Her father said nothing. Maybe he didn't want her to fly, or maybe it was too expensive. Maybe he wanted to think about it. She was too scared to ask.

Two weeks later, she worked up the nerve to bring it up again. "Dad, I want to learn to fly." To her amazement, he said, "I've been looking into that. I think the best place is Pierce's Flying Service at Baer Field." Margaret Jane was too stunned to respond. Her father continued, "A half-hour lesson is six dollars. I think you can afford that once a week. You can take the car."

"Oh, Dad, you really think I can do it?" she asked, suddenly doubtful.

"Margaret Jane, you can do anything you put your mind to." She would remember her father's words whenever she ran into tough situations.

Margaret Jane's first flying instructor, in the fall of 1941, was a young man named Dan Fry, one of three brothers who worked at Pierce's. Dan showed her the bright yellow two-seat airplane she'd be flying. Climbing in, he demonstrated how to push the control stick forward to make the nose go down, pull it back to make the nose go up, move it left to go left, and right to go right. "It's easy!" he assured her.

Dan taught Margaret Jane the basics of airplanes that day—the parts of an aircraft, the mechanics of how planes were able to fly, what controls did what and how to use them. He also explained that she would need forty hours of flying and ground-school training before she could take her flight test for a pilot's license.

The lesson over, Margaret Jane was about to go when Dan suddenly said, "Margaret Jane is an awfully long name. Do you mind if I call you Maggie?" From then on, to everyone at the airport, Margaret Jane was Maggie.

As her lessons progressed, Maggie learned, using the extra control stick in the back seat, to take over the controls when the plane was in the air. Later she learned how to read the instruments in the cockpit, how to stall the airplane by slowing the engine speed, and how to take off and land. She would soon be qualified to fly solo.

One day, when Maggie arrived for her lesson, Dan wasn't there. His older brother, Whitey, came over and told her he would be filling in. Maggie did not like Whitey very much. His gruff manner and loud cursing made her nervous.

After flying around and landing twice, Whitey climbed out of the plane and said, "You're ready to solo. Take it on out." *Solo? Today?* Maggie tried to tell him she wasn't ready, that she had not logged the required number of hours to solo. Whitey cut her off. "I said you're ready. Take it out. Now!" She did as she was told.

Maggie's first solo was exhilarating. *I'm doing it!* she thought as she glided over the landscape. She landed the craft beautifully.

When she was back on the ground, she explained to Whitey that she was not supposed to have soloed yet because she had had only six hours of instruction—the requirement was eight hours. Whitey had broken the law. He threw a fit, yelling and cursing at Maggie as if it were her fault, then stormed away.

But Maggie had soloed. And she loved it. She realized that she wanted to be a pilot, not a stewardess. She forgot about nurse's training and signed up for ground school at Indiana Technical College in Fort Wayne.

On December 7, 1941, Maggie was chatting with some friends in the airport coffee shop when the news came over the radio: the Japanese had attacked the American naval base at Pearl Harbor, Hawaii, in an air-bombing blitz. Maggie felt a pang in the pit of her stomach. The United States, she knew, was now at war.

The war caused immediate problems for private pilots. All nonmilitary flying was suspended. Every pilot had to prove that he was a U.S. citizen and renew his pilot's license with the Civilian Aeronautics Authority (CAA) before he was permitted to fly. Gas and spare engine parts became hard to get. Pilots were worried that the government might shut down all civilian flying, as Britain had already done. It was all so difficult and frustrating, Maggie thought, not to mention scary. Would she even be allowed to continue her lessons? Little did she know that the war would lead to the greatest opportunity of her life.

Even before the Pearl Harbor attack, Americans knew that the nation might be drawn into the conflict that had been raging overseas for two years, and the government took steps to prepare for that possibility. Earlier that year, the Office of Civilian Defense (OCD) had been created to prepare Americans for wartime emergencies. Only a few days before the Pearl Harbor attack, the OCD had organized the Civil Air Patrol (CAP), an association of private pilots dedicated to supporting the military in the country's defense. Among the jobs of the CAP were patroling for enemy craft; carrying out search and rescue operations; transporting cargo, mail, and personnel for the army; and keeping commercial airports open and well-maintained in case they were needed in an emergency.

The CAP was open to both male and female pilots, and Maggie was one of the first ones in Fort Wayne to sign up. The CAP provided special training, which included military-style drills and exercises. She also continued studying and practicing for the test to get her private license, and she succeeded in earning it in the summer of 1942—just in time, it turned out, for her next opportunity.

Before World War II, women could not serve in the U.S. armed forces except as nurses. As the war raged on, however, the great need for personnel persuaded the military to organize female workers in special women's auxiliary units to serve in supporting noncombat roles, thus freeing up men for combat duties. Not part of the official armed forces, these women were paid less than their male counterparts and they did not receive veterans' benefits after their service.

After the creation of the Women's Army Auxiliary Corps (WAAC) in May 1942, several women pilots, including Nancy Love and Jackie Cochran, talked to General "Hap" Arnold, the head of the Army Air Force, about starting a similar program for female pilots. These women, they suggested, would perform noncombat duties in the United States so more of the men could be sent into combat in Europe and the Pacific. By this time, the Air Force was suffering a severe shortage of qualified male pilots to fight overseas, so on September 10, 1942, General Arnold authorized the formation of the Women's Auxiliary Flying Service (WAFS), headquartered in Delaware. Five days later, the Women's Flying Training Detachment (WFTD), located in Texas, was also created.

Early in 1943, Maggie had surgery to remove her appendix. While she was at home recovering, she got the telegram asking her to interview in Chicago for the WFTD, a program she had never heard of. The other three young women pilots from Fort Wayne who received the telegram were Eugenia (Gene) Garvin, Mary McKinley, and Loretta Foellinger. The four discussed the idea. It seemed like a golden opportunity to fly lots of different airplanes and even get paid for it instead of having to pay. On February 18, the four boarded a train for Chicago, hoping to be accepted into this mysterious but exciting new program.

Although all four girls passed their interviews, Loretta could not get her parents' permission to join, and Mary failed the subsequent physical exam. Gene and Maggie, however, were ready to go and prepared to leave for Sweetwater, Texas, where they would begin their training in March.

The women pilots' program was an army secret. Maggie was allowed to tell only her immediate family where she was going and what she would be doing. The army didn't want the enemy to think they were so desperate for pilots that they had to use women.

Margaret Ray in her second-hand flight "uniform," Avenger Field, Sweetwater, Texas, 1943
—Courtesy Marsha Wright

When she reported to Sweetwater for duty with the WFTD, nicknamed "the Woofteddies," Maggie knew she would have some adjustments to make. The women pilots lived on the army base, in a bare room with six cots and twelve women to each bathroom. They had no official uniforms, but they were required to wear khaki pants with a white shirt and a khaki flight cap, all of which they had to pay for themselves. For flying, the army gave them leftover men's coveralls, which were much too large for them—they had to roll up the legs and sleeves and cinch the waist with a belt to make them fit. It was clear that "making do" would be a theme of the Woofteddies' life in the military.

Even though the women were volunteers, not officially in the army, their days were like those of any other recruit. They woke up to the sound of a bugle playing "Reveille" at 6:00 a.m., after which they had roll call, exercises, and barracks inspection. They marched in formation just about everywhere they went. They ate

Margaret standing by a PT-19A airplane, Avenger Field, Sweetwater, Texas, 1943 —Courtesy Marsha Wright

army chow, followed army rules, and could not leave the base without permission.

Half of the women's training consisted of learning to fly the many different types of military aircraft. For the other half of their day, they took classes in math, physics, meteorology, navigation, aerodynamics, electronics, military and civil air regulations, and engine operations and maintenance. When they weren't flying or attending classes, the women were studying. Maggie found no time for socializing during her six-month training period.

One day, something unusual happened to Maggie to break up her routine. A movie company wanted to make a film about the women pilots' program, and the public relations officer recommended Maggie to be in it. The filmmakers propped up the tail of a small training airplane and had Maggie climb into the cockpit. The cameraman shot from down low, so only the sky showed in the background. Maggie started the engine. With the wind from the propeller blowing her hair back, it looked like she was really flying. Maggie thought the whole thing was silly, and she never mentioned the movie, called *Silver Wings,* to anyone.

Maggie didn't think much more about it until several months later, when some other pilots asked her to join them for a movie in town. Preceding the feature was a short film called *Silver Wings.* Maggie gasped—surely this was not the same film she had been in. Suddenly, there on the screen appeared Maggie in the cockpit of a plane. One of the girls cried, "Look, Maggie, that's you!" Maggie shrank down in her seat and covered her head in embarrassment. She never did see herself in the movie. Later she said she was always sorry she hadn't looked.

The WFTD training was tough, and the trainees' flying tests were demanding. Each time they had a test, some of the students didn't pass and were immediately sent home. In Maggie's class of 127 girls, 38 dropped out, either by choice or by failing a test. Luckily, Maggie was not among them.

Near the end of her training, in August 1943, Maggie learned that the WFTD would be joined with the other women pilots' group, the

WAFS, in a new organization called the Women's Airforce Service Pilots, or WASPs. From then on, Maggie would be a WASP.

Graduation day arrived. "I cannot explain the thrill I experienced when Jackie Cochrane pinned the silver WASP wings onto my uniform," Maggie later wrote. She would cherish them forever. Her new status entitled her to be saluted as an officer, even though she was technically still a civilian volunteer.

The graduates were given their choice of assignments among several army bases. Maggie chose New Castle Army Base in Wilmington, Delaware. She would report there in a week. In the meantime, she returned to Hoagland for her sister Violet's wedding to Walter Davis. It was a simple but lovely affair at the Ray farmhouse.

At New Castle, Maggie settled into the routine of an Army Air Force pilot. She had her own room in the bachelor officers' quarters, a big improvement over the crowded barracks in Sweetwater. Each morning she would go to the "ready room" to find her day's assignment on the bulletin board. Most of the jobs were ferrying new planes from a factory to a base somewhere in the United States, although other, more dangerous tasks would also come her way. On days when she had no flying assignment, Maggie attended a training session on meteorology, navigation, or flying techniques, or she would train in a simulator.

Although Maggie had little time to herself, she enjoyed exchanging letters with the folks back in Indiana. One of her pen pals was a serviceman from her church named Morris Ringenberg. One day Maggie and two other WASPs were assigned to fly to Hagerstown, Maryland, where Morris happened to be stationed at the time. When they arrived, Maggie called him up, and he offered to take the three ladies to dinner. "It was fun seeing someone from home," she later recalled, "but I thought of him strictly as a friend." Maggie would not see Morris again until the war was over and they were both back home.

In November the WASP pilots finally received official uniforms. They were quite sharp-looking: a belted jacket and skirt, a short jacket and pants, and a beret-style hat, all of rich Santiago blue.

A blue or white shirt with a black tie completed the uniform. The WASPs had to pay for their uniforms with their own money, and they were expensive. But like most of the other women, Maggie felt it was worth it to have a real uniform that fit. She slipped into the jacket and proudly pinned on her insignia and her silver wings.

Some of the missions WASPs flew were much more dangerous than most people thought. Not only did they ferry planes from factories to army bases, they also towed targets for artillery and anti-aircraft gunners to practice shooting at with live ammunition. One of the riskiest assignments was transporting old, worn-out planes to be scrapped—because these planes were deemed no longer airworthy, pilots never knew if they would make it to their destination.

Even simple practice flights had their dangers. Maggie had heard about a few fatal crashes, but she didn't know any of the victims until one day in 1943. She had been sent to Brownsville, Texas, for special training in fighter planes, known as pursuit planes. A group was practicing flying in formation when one of the pursuits accidentally struck another's wing tip, sending both planes spinning to the ground. Two students and an instructor, all of whom Maggie knew, were killed in the crash.

Even when a WASP was killed, the army did not pay her survivors any benefits. Her coffin would not be draped with a flag, nor did her family receive a gold star banner, representing a service member killed in action. The army didn't even pay for the body to be shipped home. All because WASPs were not regular army soldiers. During World War II, WASP pilots served at 120 air bases, ferried 12,650 airplanes of 78 different types over 60 million miles. Thirty-eight WASP fliers lost their lives in the course of their service.

Maggie had her own narrow escape early in 1944. She was transferring a worn-out twin-engine Cessna AT-17 Bobcat, a model nicknamed the "Bamboo Bomber" for its lightweight canvas-and-plywood construction, from Bradley Field in Connecticut to Montgomery, Alabama, where the plane would be put out of service.

Near Washington, D.C., the plane started shaking and making a rumbling sound. Maggie eased up on the gas, but the shaking got worse. She shut down the left engine and restarted it, but it only sputtered—it was ready to fail. The vibrations continued. Maggie knew she was in trouble. She called the nearest airport and told the control tower she had a problem. Now she was losing altitude. The tower operator responded that the Cessna was not worth saving— she should bail out with her parachute and let the plane crash.

Maggie scanned the ground below her. It was mostly open fields and woods with few buildings. She tightened her parachute harness and prepared to climb between the seats and jump out the rear door. She would leave the engines running until the last moment, to keep the plane level for her jump. Just before she jumped, she would lean over the seat and cut off the engines, letting the airplane crash, hopefully in a safe place.

Maggie hesitated. She was not afraid to jump, but she knew that allowing an unguided airplane to crash was dangerous. It could injure or kill unseen people or start a forest fire. She was still in control of the aircraft and believed she could land it. Again checking the instrument panel, she took a deep breath and decided that piloting a landing was the safest choice. Back on the radio, she told the control tower she was going to land, giving the operator her location and altitude. Now she could see the airport. She told the tower she was coming straight in.

The Cessna was bouncing wildly, and Maggie had to use all her strength to control it. The wheels touched down with less of a jolt than Maggie expected, and she eased the broken plane down the runway. She had done it! The craft was still rolling and the engines still running when she noticed a fire truck and ambulance rushing toward her. Looking forward, she saw gas pouring out over her left engine. It could catch fire and blow up at any second. With the plane still moving, she immediately shut off the engines, rushed to the back door, and jumped out. Maggie had seen her share of close calls, but this was the closest one yet.

The base commander picked Maggie up in his jeep and told her she had done a great job of landing the craft. In the commander's office, Maggie, still shaken up, called the safety officer at her home base to report the incident. She told him there was no damage to the plane other than the blown engine. But the safety officer started yelling and cursing at her for disobeying orders. After all she had just gone through, she couldn't take his scolding. She turned away from the phone and let her tears fall while the safety officer kept yelling.

The commander, listening to the exchange, took the phone out of Maggie's hand and asked the safety officer for his name, rank, and serial number. He was taking her side, knowing she had used good common sense and had saved the aircraft from crashing. Then the commander told Maggie to stay on his base that night and take the next day off.

A few weeks later, Maggie was assigned to fly an officer to Savannah, Georgia, where he would be reporting for overseas duty. She was taken aback when she saw that the man was the rude safety officer who had chewed her out. He didn't speak to her the entire way. Maggie felt bad, not for herself but for him, wondering if he was being sent into the war zone because of the way he had treated her.

By December of 1944, the war was slowing down. Maggie and the other WASPs were shocked and dismayed to learn that the government had suddenly decided to end the WASP program. Maggie and the 914 other WASP fliers still on active duty were to be dismissed on December 20. That was it. It was all over. Would Maggie ever be able to fly again?

After the war, soldiers in the regular Army, all 8.8 million of them, received many veterans' benefits, including low-interest mortgages and business loans, free medical care, and cash payments to attend the school of their choice, as well as one year of unemployment compensation. But WASP pilots did not enjoy any of those benefits. All records from the WASP program were sealed as official secrets for the next thirty-five years.

After the WASPs were disbanded, Maggie signed up for the Air Force Reserve as a first lieutenant. Until (or unless) she was called back into service with the reserve, she would need a job. Commercial airlines hired only male pilots, and there were few other civilian jobs for flyers, especially for women flyers, who were generally passed over in favor of men. But Maggie was determined to fly.

Back in Indiana, Maggie picked up a few ferrying jobs, but she could find nothing permanent. She talked to her friend Fred Bunyan, who told her he was going to buy Pierce's Flying Service, the place where Maggie had learned to fly. After receiving her instructor's rating in March, she worked there as a private flight instructor. But when students came to the airport to take flying lessons, they usually didn't want a female instructor. Sometimes, though, Maggie took over for an absent male instructor, and after they flew with her, the students often stayed with her.

By early August 1945, an Allied victory was at hand. Germany had surrendered, and Japan was expected to soon follow suit. Both of the Fort Wayne newspapers happened to be on strike at the time, so a local radio news station, WGL, wanting to be the first to announce the good news, called Pierce Flying Service, asking for a pilot to drop pamphlets announcing V-J Day and the end of World War II. When the announcement came on August 14, Maggie flew a Piper Cub while an assistant dropped the leaflets over the downtown streets and parking lots.

In August of 1995, a few days before the fiftieth anniversary of the war's end, Maggie happened to be listening to WGL when someone mentioned the leaflets and asked if anyone listening had information about the pilot of the plane that had dropped them. Maggie called in and said, "That was me!" The station hired her to drop the same leaflets again for the anniversary. Maggie called it "frosting on the cake."

After the war ended, Morris Ringenberg came home to Fort Wayne with a Purple Heart medal. He became a banker. At church, Maggie and Morris became reacquainted, and they started getting together to share stories of the war, local news, and childhood memories. By Christmas, they were dating, and the following summer they got engaged. Maggie was still called Margaret Jane by her family, but Morris called her Margaret, and she decided to go by Margaret from then on.

The couple's small, simple wedding took place in October of 1946 at Morris's parents' house. The groom's father, a minister, performed the ceremony. The newlyweds moved into an apartment in a building that Margaret's father owned. The following year, the Ringenbergs welcomed their first child, Marsha, and moved into a house in Grabill.

Margaret continued flying and giving lessons, leaving Marsha with Margaret's mom or a babysitter. When Marsha was a little older, Margaret sometimes took the tot with her in the plane. Morris was not a pilot, but Margaret would later teach him enough for him to be her copilot on occasion. Marsha would grow up to be a flyer like her mother, though not as a profession.

In 1951, with the Korean War under way, Margaret got the call from the Army Reserve, asking her to go on active duty as a captain. She sent a letter saying that she could serve, but it had to be near her home, since she now had a small child. The response came, saying that as a woman with a child under eighteen, she could not serve. Such a rule did not apply to men, of course. Margaret was discharged.

Margaret and Morris's second child, a boy they named Mike, came along in 1953. The Ringenbergs moved again, to a larger house next door to a pilot with his own plane and his own landing strip, both of which he generously allowed Margaret to borrow for giving lessons. This allowed her to spend more time with her children. By all accounts, Margaret was a loving and devoted mother. In later years, no matter how busy she was, she always insisted that the whole family gather to share a meal every Sunday.

In 1956 the Indiana chapter of the Ninety-Nines, an international association of women pilots, helped sponsor the annual All Woman Transcontinental Air Race, nicknamed the Powder Puff Derby. Margaret, a member of the Ninety-Nines, was on hand to help direct the planes landing in Fort Wayne, an official stop that year. With two small children and a tight budget, Margaret had not thought of entering this race herself, but seeing the contestants flying in and out planted a seed in her mind.

The seed grew, and Margaret decided to try to enter the next Powder Puff Derby. There were numerous expenses involved and a thousand details to attend to, from finding a plane to picking out clothes for herself and her copilot—the rules required they dress in matching outfits—dresses or skirts and blouses, no slacks.

Margaret submitted her entry application and fee, found a plane to borrow, and with Morris's sister Lois agreeing to copilot, made all the necessary plans. As the date approached, however, Lois's mother became gravely ill, so Lois had to drop out. Margaret was going to drop out, too, but her family encouraged her to stay in. A friend named Marty Wyall, who like Margaret was a former WASP, volunteered to take Lois's place. Luckily, she fit into Lois's dress.

Airplane racing is not like car racing, where each driver tries to go as fast as he can, all at the same time. The goals in airplane racing are more complicated. In some races, the idea is to use the least amount of fuel; in others, it is trying to get as close as possible to one's own estimate of the time a trip will take; still others have different rules. Racers use different planes with various weights, construction, and capabilities, so scores are based on complex formulas. The first pilot to land is seldom the winner.

In the middle of the race, which that year went from San Carlos, California, to Philadelphia, Margaret learned during a stopover that her mother-in-law had died. Morris insisted she finish the race. In the end, Margaret and Marty were disqualified for a minor rule infraction, but they had finished. Margaret raced in the Powder Puff Derby every year from then on, all the way up to the year of her death. In 1976 the official title of the race was changed to the Air Race Classic; although the words "All Woman" were taken out of the title, it remained a women's race and continues to be that today.

Margaret usually finished in the top ten in the Air Race Classic, though she won first place only once, in 1988. She also competed regularly in the Fairladies' Annual Indiana Race (FAIR), as well as a number of smaller races. Although she always said she raced more for fun than to win, by the end of her career, she had won enough trophies, ribbons, and awards to fill two rooms in her house.

Margaret loved to talk about her racing adventures, remembering all the people she met and the fun she had. She experienced her share of mishaps and challenges, from radio malfunctions to encounters with bad weather to engine failure. But friends say that no matter how serious the problem was, Margaret was "never rattled."

Over the years, Margaret's copilots were often family members, including Morris and her daughter, Marsha. When Marsha was a Senior Girl Scout, her troop decided to learn to fly. The girls earned their tuition for ground school by cleaning up around the hangars. Three of the girls, including Marsha, earned private pilot's licenses. In later years, Marsha was sometimes her mother's competitor. Eventually Margaret taught all of her grandchildren how to copilot and flew with them in races.

Margaret's greatest race adventure was in 1994, when she flew around the world in a twenty-four-day, coed race sponsored by the International Civil Aviation Organization. Margaret was asked to participate by a doctor from California who called her in 1993, saying he had heard some pilots mention her name. "I'm told you're one of the best," he said. He had a plane, and he wanted Margaret to be his copilot. She had never flown over the ocean before. It was a terrifying prospect, but that did not stop her from saying yes. At the time, Margaret was seventy-two.

With so much racing experience, Margaret was an old hand at making preparations, but she'd never had to plan for a monthlong, international race. In addition to everything else, she needed a passport, visas, and innoculations. She had to study the race's complex rules and learn what she could about overseas flying.

Only a couple of weeks before the race, the doctor dropped out after suffering a stroke. Margaret now had to find a copilot with all the requirements and paperwork needed for the race. She called everyone she could think of, but no one could do it, so she called the race director to tell him she was dropping out. But the director had an idea. He said he knew two Canadian pilots who wanted to race but could not find a plane. Margaret called the pilots, named Adele and Daphne, and they both agreed to team up with Margaret.

After dealing with several last-minute mechanical issues with the plane, Margaret, Adele, and Daphne took off on May 1, 1994, from Montreal, Canada. The race would take them 15,000 miles across the Atlantic Ocean through Morocco, Turkey, the United Arab Emirates, India, Thailand, Vietnam, Japan, Siberia, and Alaska, ending back in Montreal. During the trip, they dealt with a radio malfunction, a typhoon, gas shortages, and food poisoning. They finished in last place, but they felt like winners.

After her race around the world, Margaret received many invitations to speak. At first, public speaking frightened her more than flying. But she grew into a comfortable and enthusiastic speaker and became something of a celebrity. One of her greatest honors, she said, was speaking to cadets at the United States Air Force Academy in 1998. The audience responded to her talk with a standing ovation.

In 1998 Margaret wrote her "aerobiography," titled *Girls Can't Be Pilots*. That same year, Tom Brokaw devoted an entire chapter in his bestselling book *The Greatest Generation* to Margaret Ray Ringenberg. The following year, she was presented with the National Aeronautic Association's Elder Statesman in Aviation Award in Washington, D.C.

Margaret made headlines when in 2001, at age seventy-nine, she flew in a race from London, England, to Sydney, Australia. The next year, she was named one of Indiana's six "Living Legends." The same year, 2002, on a visit to NASA, she joined an astronaut in the space shuttle simulator, which she piloted perfectly.

After her beloved husband, Morris Ringenberg, died in 2003, Margaret continued to race, often with one of her five grandchildren as copilot. She was honored in 2006 when she was invited to represent the WASPs at the dedication of the Air Force Memorial in Washington, D.C. In 2007, Marsha Ringenberg Wright wrote and published a book about her mother's days as a WASP called *Maggie*

Ray: World War II Air Force Pilot. Early in 2008, Margaret learned that she was to be inducted into the Women in Aviation Hall of Fame.

At age eighty-seven, Margaret flew in what was to be her final race, the 2008 Air Race Classic. She finished third. About a month later, in July, she attended the Experimental Aircraft Association's annual "Fly-in Convention" and air show in Oshkosh, Wisconsin, where she and several other former WASPs had been asked to speak. On average, half a million visitors from sixty countries attend "The World's Greatest Aviation Celebration" each year. Maggie was delighted to be there, reunited with her old friends, looking at airplanes and talking about flying.

The WASP ladies had agreed to meet for breakfast at their hotel on the morning of their talk. As the women sat there with their coffee, they wondered why Maggie was so late in joining them. It wasn't like her. A short time later, they were shocked and deeply saddened to learn that she had died quietly in her sleep. It was a bittersweet end for Margaret Ray Ringenberg, as she passed away during a celebration among her fellow pilots.

Margaret's obituary appeared in numerous national newspapers and magazines, calling her an "aviation pioneer," "a flying legend," and "a true American hero." Services, attended by more than two hundred mourners, were held at the Grabill Missionary Church. At the memorial, one article said, "tears often gave way to laughter as cherished memories were shared."

Years after her death, Margaret was not forgotten. In 2013 the Public Broadcasting System aired a documentary about her career called *Wings for Maggie Ray.*

At the United States Air Force Academy in 1998, Margaret had shared with the cadets her personal philosophy: "Though the course you're on may change headings along the way, just remember—the sky's the limit, your future's bright, and it's not where you've come from, but where you are going that counts. Aim high!"

SELECTED SOURCES

1. TACUMWAH, CATES, AND KILSOQUAH

Cayton, Andrew R. L. *Frontier Indiana*. Bloomington: Indiana University Press, 1996.

Dunn, Jacob Piatt. *True Indian Stories*. Indianapolis: Sentinel, 1908.

Lid, Enid. "Story of the life of Indian woman who is now over 100 years of age." *Auburn Courier*, June 28, 1909.

Moore, Perry G. "History of the Anthony Wayne Flag." Indianapolis: Indiana Historical Bureau, 1904.

Pherson, Alan J. and Carr, James. *Notable American Indians: Indiana and Adjacent States*. Bloomington, IN: Authorhouse, 2007.

Rafert, Stewart. *The Hidden Community: The Miami Indians of Indiana, 1846–1940*. PhD diss., University of Delaware, 1982.

———. *The Miami Indians of Indiana: A Persistent People, 1654–1994*. Indianapolis: Indiana Historical Society Press, 1996.

Reading, Nellie. "Kilsoquah." Address to the Antiquestor Club. http://roanoke.lib.in.us/history/kilsoquah/nellie-reddings-account-of-kilsoquah/. Accessed May 28, 2015.

Shoemaker, Scott Michael. *Trickster Skins: Narratives of Landscape, Representation, and the Miami Nation*. PhD diss., University of Minnesota, 2011.

2. MARIE BAILLY

Altrocchi, Julia Cooley. *Wolves Against the Moon*. (Novel loosely based on the life of Joseph Bailly). New York: MacMillan, 1940.

Bowers, John O. *The Old Bailly Homestead*. Gary, IN: 1922.

Costello, Joan, and Betty Canright. "The Bailly Women." Paper presented to Duneland Historical Society at Chesterton Library Service Center, Chesterton, Indiana, February 21, 2002.

Federal Writers Project. *Calumet Region Historical Guide*. Gary, IN: Board of Education of Gary, 1939.

Howe, Frances R. *Story of a French Homestead in the Old Northwest*. Reprint, Bowie, MD: Heritage Books, 1999.

Moore, Powell A. *The Calumet Region, Indiana's Last Frontier*. Indianapolis: Indiana Historical Bureau, 1959.

Schiemann, Olga Mae. *From a Bailly Point of View*. Chesterton, IN: Duneland Historical Society, 1955.

3. MOTHER THÉODORE GUÉRIN

Burton, Catherine. *Faith is the Substance: the Life of Mother Theodore Guerin*. St. Louis: Herder, 1959.

Cebula, Judith. "Trailblazing Faith." *Indianapolis Star Extra*, July 23, 1997.

Mitchell, Penny Blaker. *Mother Theodore Guerin: A Woman for Our Time: Foundress of the Sisters of Providence of Saint Mary-of-the-Woods, Indiana*. Saint Mary-of-the-Woods, IN: Sisters of Providence, 1998.

Mug, Sr. Mary Theodosia. *Journals and Letters of Mother Theodore Guerin*. Saint Mary-of-the-Woods, IN: Providence Press, 1937.

Sisters of Providence. "Saint Mother Theodore Guerin." spsmw.org/saint-mother-theodore-guerin/.

Young, Julie. *A Belief in Providence: A Life of Saint Theodora Guerin*. Indianapolis: Indiana Historical Society Press, 2007.

4. SARAH BOLTON

Ball Center for Creative Inquiry. "Sarah T. Barrett Bolton." http://landandlit.iweb.bsu.edu/Literature/Authors/boltonsb.html. Accessed September 24, 2015.

Bolton, Sarah T. *Life and Poems of Sarah T. Bolton*. Indianapolis: Fred L. Horton & Co., 1880.

———. *Paddle Your Own Canoe and Other Poems*. Edited by John Clark Ridpath. Indianapolis: Bowen-Merrill, 1897.

Downing, Olive Inez. *Indiana's Poet of the Wildwood*. Marion, IN: News Publishing Company, 1941.

Dunn, Jacob Piatt. *Greater Indianapolis*. Chicago: Lewis Publishing, 1910.

Hays, Clifford E. "Sarah T. Bolton (1814–1893): Indiana's First Poet." Poet's Corner Poetry Club newsletter, Indianapolis, 1978.

5. ZERELDA WALLACE

Britton, Bonnie. "Susan Anthony Helped Women Get Vote Right." *Indianapolis Star*, November 7, 1971.

Post, Margaret Moore. *First Ladies of Indiana and the Governors, 1816–1984*. Indianapolis: privately published, 1984.

"Recognizing Zerelda G. Wallace and her leadership." *Journal Review*. http://www.journalreview.com/opinion/article_f635377a-fa07-11e2-aea8-001a4bcf887a.html. Accessed September 19, 2013.

Rose, Ernestine Bradford. "Early Leaders of Women." *Indianapolis Star Magazine*, March 28, 1976.

Sloan, L. Alene. *Some Aspects of the Woman Suffrage Movement in Indiana.* PhD diss., Ball State University, 1982.

Vogelgesang, Susan. "Zerelda Wallace, Indiana's Conservative Radical." *Traces of Indiana and Midwestern History* 4, no. 3.

Willard, Frances Elizabeth, and Mary Ashton Rice Livermore. *A Woman of the Century: Fourteen Hundred-seventy [sic] Biographical Sketches Accompanied by Portraits of Women in All Walks of Life.* Buffalo, NY: Moulton, 1893.

"Woman Suffrage History Recalled in Anniversary: Right to Vote for Mothers and Daughters Will be Five Years Old Wednesday." *Indianapolis Star,* August 23, 1925.

6. LILLIAN THOMAS FOX

Ferguson, Earline Rae. "The Woman's Improvement Club of Indianapolis: Black Women Pioneers in Tuberculosis Work, 1903–1938." *Indiana Magazine of History* 80, no. 3 (September 1984).

Gibbs, Wilma, ed. *Indiana's African American Heritage: Essays from Black History News and Notes.* Indianapolis: Indiana Historical Society, 1993.

Grahn, Anya. *The Rise and Fall of the Tuberculosis Sanatorium in Response to the White Plague.* Master's thesis, Ball State University, 2012.

Indiana Magazine of History staff. "Above and Beyond: Lillian Thomas Fox and Beulah Wright Porter." A Moment of Indiana History. http://indianapublicmedia.org/momentofindianahistory/lillian-thomas-fox-beulah-wright-porter/. Accessed January 1, 2014.

Slaymaker, Julie. "Lillian Thomas Fox." Indiana Journalism Hall of Fame. http://indianajournalismhof.org/2014/04/fox-lillian-thomas/.

Toler, Frances A. *Lillian Thomas Fox: Black Woman Journalist of Indiana.* Master's thesis, Ball State University, 1978.

7. GENE STRATTON-PORTER

Ball Center for Creative Inquiry. "Gene Stratton-Porter." http://landandlit.iweb.bsu.edu/Literature/Authors/portergs.htm. Accessed November 3, 2007.

Encyclopaedia Britannica. "Gene Stratton Porter." http://www.britannica com/EBchecked/topic/471100/Gene-Stratton-Porter. Accessed December 11, 2007.

"Gene Stratton Porter." *The Indiana Historian,* September 1996.

Eldridge, Ann, and Nancy Carlson. *Gene Stratton Porter: Voice of the Limberlost.* Video. Ball State University, 1996.

Long, Judith Reick. *Gene Stratton Porter, Novelist and Naturalist.* Indianapolis: Indiana Historical Society, 1990.

Meehan, Jeannette Porter. *Lady of the Limberlost: The Life and Letters of Gene Stratton Porter.* Mattituck, NY: Amereon House, 1972.

8. THE OVERBECK SISTERS

Denker, Ellen Paul. "Creating a Life: The Overbeck Sisters and Their Cambridge City Pottery." *Traces of Indiana and Midwestern History,* Spring 2005.

Gaffney, Dennis. "Next of Kiln: The Overbeck Sisters." Antiques Roadshow, Houston, 2006. http://www.pbs.org/wgbh/roadshow/fts/houston_200503A35.html. Accessed October 26, 2006.

Johnson, Don. "Overbeck Pottery." *Today's Collector,* October 1994.

Newton, Judith Vale, and Carol Ann Weiss. *Skirting the Issue: Stories of Indiana's Historical Women Artists.* Indianapolis: Indiana Historical Society Press, 2004.

Overbeck Museum. http://www.cclib.lib.in.us/overbeck-museum/4571990690. Accessed August 5, 2006.

Postle, Kathleen R. *The Chronicle of the Overbeck Pottery.* Indianapolis: Indiana Historical Society Press, 1978.

Richert, Natalie. *The Overbeck Sisters: A Legacy of Spirit.* Video. Natalie Richert Productions, 2004.

Waynet.org. "The Overbeck Sisters." http://www.waynet.org/ency/artist/bio/overbeck-sisters.htm. Accessed September 24, 2015.

9. MADAM C. J. WALKER

Brodie, James Michael. *Created Equal: The Lives and Ideas of Black American Innovators.* New York: William Morrow, 1993.

Bundles, A'Lelia. *Madam C. J. Walker, Entrepreneur.* Philadelphia: Chelsea House, 1991.

——. *On Her Own Ground: The Life and Times of Madam C. J. Walker.* New York: Scribner, 2001.

Gates, Henry Louis, Jr. "Madam Walker: The First Black American Woman to Be a Self-made Millionaire." http://www.pbs.org/wnet/african-americans-many-rivers-to-cross/history/100-amazing-facts/madam-walker-the-first-black-american-woman-to-be-a-self-made-millionaire/.

Lomel, Cookie. *Madam C. J. Walker, Entrepreneur.* Los Angeles: Melrose Square Publishing, 1993.

"Madam C. J. Walker." *Indiana Junior Historian,* February and March 1992.

10. DOROTHY BUELL

Engel, J. Ronald. *Sacred Sands: The Struggle for Community in the Indiana Dunes.* Scranton, PA: Wesleyan University Press, 1983.

Franklin, Kay. *Duel for the Dunes: Land Use Conflict on the Shores of Lake Michigan*. Urbana: University of Illinois Press, 1963.

Greenberg, Joel. *A Natural History of the Chicago Region*. Chicago: University of Chicago Press, 2002.

National Park Service. "Indiana Dunes National Lakeshore." http://www.nps.gov/indu/index.htm. Accessed April 24, 2014.

Peeples, William. "The Indiana Dunes and Pressure Politics." *Atlantic Monthly*, February 1963.

Read, Herb. "Portraits in Time." *Singing Sands Almanac*, Spring 2005.

Schoon, Kenneth J. *Dreams of Duneland*. Bloomington, IN: Quarry Books, Indiana University Press, 2013.

11. VIVIAN CARTER

Callahan, Mike. "The Vee-Jay Story." http://www.bsnpubs.com/veejay/veejaystory1.html. Accessed March 25, 2015.

Garofalo, Reebee. "Crossing Over: From Black Rhythm and Blues to White Rock 'n' Roll." In *Rhythm and Business: The Political Economy of Black Music*. Pdf. http://www.lipscomb.umn.edu/rock/docs/Garofalo2002_crossingOver. Accessed April 23, 2015.

Kostanczuk, Bob. "Found and Lost: How a Legendary Band Got Away from a Gary-born Record Label." *Gary Post-Tribune*, August 23, 1998.

Lane, James B. "Vivian Carter and Vee Jay Records." In *Gary's First Hundred Years: A Centennial History of Gary Indiana 1906–2006*. Valparaiso, IN: Home Mountain Printing, 2006.

——— "Vivian Carter and Vee Jay Records." *Traces of Indiana and Midwestern History*, Winter 2011.

Pruter, Robert. *Chicago Soul*. Urbana: University of Illinois Press, 1991.

12. MARGARET RAY RINGENBERG

Brokaw, Tom. "Margaret Ray Ringenberg." In *The Greatest Generation*. New York: Delta, 1998.

Paluso, Philip M., producer. "Wings for Maggie Ray." PBS television documentary, 2013.

Ringenberg, Margaret J., with Jane L. Roth. *Girls Can't Be Pilots: An Aerobiography*. Fort Wayne, IN: Daedalus Press, 1998.

Wright, Marsha J. *Maggie Ray: World War II Air Force Pilot*. Bloomington, IN: Pen and Publish, 2007.

SITES TO VISIT

TACUMWAH, CATES, AND KILSOQUAH

Forks of the Wabash Historic Park: This museum park near Huntington, Indiana, features several historic buildings, trails, and remnants of the Wabash and Erie Canal. The park is located along the Wabash River, at the place where Kilsoquah was born. The former home of Chief Richardville (5705 Bluffton Rd.) is a major attraction at the park. Call ahead to arrange a tour. Forks of the Wabash Historic Park, 3011 West Park Drive, Huntington, IN 46750; (260) 356-1903; http://visithuntington.org/attractions/forks-of-the-wabash-historic-park.

History Center: Home of the Allen County-Fort Wayne Historical Society. History Center, 302 E. Barry St., Fort Wayne, IN 46802; (260) 426-2882; http://www.fwhistorycenter.com/aboutUs.html.

Websites:
http://www.miamiindians.org/
http://www.bigorrin.org/miami_kids.htm
http://www.digplanet.com/wiki/Tacumwah
http://historycenterfw.blogspot.com/2012/08/tacumwah-18th-century-people-magazine.html
http://www.findagrave.com/cgi-bin/fg.cgi?page=gr&GRid=42524979
http://roanoke.lib.in.us/history/kilsoquah/

MARIE BAILLY

Bailly Homestead at Indiana Dunes National Lakeshore: The Homestead near Chesterton, Indiana, brings together an unusual combination of folk architecture, with rustic log and brick structures, and late 19th-century architecture of the imposing main house, along with the family cemetery. Other attractions are nearby. Start at the Indiana Dunes National Lakeshore Visitor Center, US Highway 20 at Indiana Highway 49, Porter, IN 46304; (219) 395-1882; http://www.nps.gov/indu/learn/historyculture/bailly_homestead.htm.

Websites:
http://www.inportercounty.org/Data/Cemeteries/BaillyCemetery.html
https://en.wikipedia.org/wiki/Joseph_Bailly_Homestead

MOTHER THÉODORE GUÉRIN

Shrine of Saint Mother Theodore Guerin: This shrine, the final resting place of Mother Theodore Guerin (Saint Theodora), has been designed to represent her journey from France to Saint Mary-of-the-Woods, Indiana, near Terre Haute. The site offers tours and has a gift shop. Shrine of Saint Mother Theodore Guerin, Sisters of Providence Road, Saint Mary-of-the-Woods, IN 47876; (812) 535-3131; http://spsmw.org/saint-mother-theodore/the-shrine-of-saint-mother-theodore-guerin/.

Websites:
http://spsmw.org/saint-mother-theodore/
https://en.wikipedia.org/wiki/Th%C3%A9odore_Gu%C3%A9rin
http://www.catholic.org/saints/saint.php?saint_id=6984
https://en.wikipedia.org/wiki/Saint_Mary-of-the-Woods,_Indiana

SARAH BOLTON

Sarah T. Bolton Park: Located in Beech Grove, this park was established on the grounds of Sarah's final home, though the house itself is gone. Sarah T. Bolton Park, Sherman Drive (17th Avenue) and Main Street, Beech Grove, IN 46107; (317) 788-4977; http://www.beechgrove.com/sarah-t-bolton-park.html

Indiana Medical History Museum: Interestingly, the Indiana Medical History Museum in Indianapolis was built on the grounds of Sarah and Nathaniel Bolton's farm, tavern, and first home, which became Central State Hospital in 1845 before becoming a museum. Indiana Medical History Museum, 3045 W. Vermont St., Indianapolis, IN 46222; (317) 635-7329; http://www.imhm.org/.

You can also see the 1941 bronze image of Sarah Bolton, which includes a few lines from her poem "Indiana," on the second-floor rotunda of the Indiana State Capitol in Indianapolis.

Websites:
http://www.beechgrove.com/sarah-t-bolton.html
http://inpolicy.org/2014/08/indiana-at-200-31-paddle-your-own-canoe/

ZERELDA WALLACE

General Lew Wallace Study and Museum. Get the flavor of Zerelda's times by visiting the Interpretive Center and National Historic Landmark building designed by her famous stepson, Lew Wallace, who was a Civil War general, the governor of the New Mexico Territory, and the author of the novel *Ben-Hur*. Not much information about Zerelda here, but it's still worth a visit. General Lew Wallace Study and Museum, 200 Wallace Ave., Crawfordsville, IN 47933; 765-362-5769; http://www.ben-hur.com/.

Websites
http://www.journalreview.com/opinion/article_a1c358ee-3bb8-11e5-ad2b-b349aa09709c.html

http://www.journalreview.com/opinion/article_f910582c-dc48-11e1-
  8255-0019bb2963f4.html

https://en.wikipedia.org/wiki/Zerelda_G._Wallace

http://www.ben-hur.com/category/wallace-family/zerelda-wallace/

LILLIAN THOMAS FOX

Websites:

http://indianajournalismhof.org/2014/04/fox-lillian-thomas/

http://indianapublicmedia.org/momentofindianahistory/lillian-thomas-fox-
  beulah-wright-porter/

https://en.wikipedia.org/wiki/Lillian_Thomas_Fox

http://cardinalscholar.bsu.edu/handle/handle/186063

GENE STRATTON-PORTER

There are two main places to learn more about Gene Stratton-Porter's life.
Separated by eighty miles, they are both worth a visit.

Limberlost State Historic Site: Limberlost Cabin, Gene's earlier home in
Geneva, south of Fort Wayne, is preserved as an Indiana State Historic Site,
and Limberlost Swamp is now a nature preserve and has been partially
restored, thanks to Indiana's 1996 Wetlands Conservation Plan. Limberlost
State Historic Site, 202 East 6th Street, Geneva, IN 46740; (260) 368-7428;
http://limberlost.weebly.com/.

Gene Stratton-Porter State Historic Site: Gene's later home, Wildflower
Woods in Rome City, northwest of Fort Wayne, is also a nature preserve
and public museum, operated by the Indiana State Museum system.
Gene Stratton-Porter State Historic Site, 1205 Pleasant Point, Rome City,
IN 4678; (260) 854-3790; http://www.genestratton-porter.com; see also
http://www.indianamuseum.org/explore/gene-stratton-porter-home.

Websites:

http://www.indianahistory.org/our-collections/reference/notable-
  hoosiers/gene-stratton-porter#.VgW91GRVhHw

http://genestratton-porter.org/

https://en.wikipedia.org/wiki/Gene_Stratton-Porter

http://www.online-literature.com/stratton-porter/

http://landandlit.iweb.bsu.edu/Literature/Authors/portergs.htm

THE OVERBECK SISTERS

Overbeck Museum: Located on the ground floor of the Cambridge City
Public Library, the museum preserves the creative art of the Overbeck
sisters, who lived and worked in Cambridge City. Overbeck Museum,
Cambridge City Public Library, 600 West Main Street, Cambridge

City, IN 47327; (765) 478-3335; http://www.cclib.lib.in.us/overbeck-museum/4571990690.

Overbeck House: Now a private home; visits by appointment only. Overbeck House, 520 E. Church St., Cambridge City, IN 47327; (765) 478-5993; http://www.waynet.org/waynet/spotlight/2001/010723-overbeckhouse.htm.

Websites:
http://www.waynet.org/nonprofit/overbeck.htm
http://www.pbs.org/wgbh/roadshow/fts/houston_200503A35.html

MADAM C. J. WALKER

Madam Walker Theatre Center: This block-long building in downtown Indianapolis was originally the home of the Walker Manufacturing plant, where Madame C. J. Walker's hair-care products were produced and distributed. Upon opening in 1927, the factory building also boasted a movie theatre, a pharmacy, a beauty salon, and a beauty school. It is now an African American cultural center that includes a small museum dedicated to Madam Walker. Madam Walker Theatre Center, 617 Indiana Avenue, Indianapolis, IN 46202; (317) 236-2099; http://www.thewalkertheatre.org/.

Websites:
http://www.madamcjwalker.com/#&panel1-1
http://www.biography.com/people/madam-cj-walker-9522174

DOROTHY BUELL

Indiana Dunes National Lakeshore: See the unique landscape that Dorothy and thousands of volunteers worked for fifty years to save, near Chesterton. Visit Chellberg Farm, Cowles' Bog historic ecology site, and a cluster of five "houses of tomorrow" saved from Chicago's 1933 Century of Progress World's Fair and barged across Lake Michigan in 1935. Start at the visitor's center. Indiana Dunes National Lakeshore Visitor Center, 1215 N. State Highway 49 (at US 20), Porter, IN 46304; (219) 926-2255; http://www.nps.gov/indu/planyourvisit/idnlvc.htm.

Websites:
http://savedunes.org/about/our-history/
https://www.facebook.com/savedunes

VIVIAN CARTER

Sadly, Vivian's record store in Gary no longer exists, nor does Vee-Jay headquarters.

Websites:
http://www.veejayrecords.net/

http://www.bsnpubs.com/veejay/veejaystory1.html
http://www.npr.org/templates/story/story.php?storyId=18112344

MARGARET RAY RINGENBERG

There are no historical sites in Hoagland related to Margaret, but you can visit the National WASP World War II Museum in Sweetwater, Texas. National WASP World War II Museum, 210 Loop 170, Sweetwater, TX 79556; (325) 235-0099; http://waspmuseum.org/.

Websites:

http://twudigital.contentdm.oclc.org/cdm/landingpage/collection/p214coll2

http://dictionary.sensagent.com/WOMEN%20AIRFORCE%20SERVICE%20PILOTS/en-en/

https://www.wai.org/pioneers/2008pioneers.cfm

INDEX

Page numbers in italics indicate illustrations.

LOUISE HILLERY has lived most of her life in Indiana. After teaching students with special needs in the public schools, she taught mathematics at a community college and began a project to learn about the women of Indiana history, which resulted in this book. She is an active musician in her community of Columbus and a composer of music for the bassoon. She is most proud of her two sons and especially dotes on her two grandsons.